PRAISE FOR

▼

TAHOE BOY

Pat Hickey takes the reader on a remarkable odyssey from America's Alpine peaks to the Pacific Rim and finds what everyone is searching for—grand and daring adventure, the love of his life and sacred peace. The book is a fascinating companion for all who love a good story by a writer who has lived his life with imagination, courage and a great number of surprises including deep happiness through, all things, an arranged marriage via a beautiful photograph in an envelope. You will be telling your family and friends about this fascinating book.

—**WARREN LERUDE**, Pulitzer Prize winning author

A classic coming-of-age story from the wild 1960's to the fulfillment of a spiritual quest. Local color, sparkling anecdotes, humor and the true speed of a picturesque novel makes this book a must read.

—**MOSE DURST, PH. D.,** Former President of the Unification Church

In *Tahoe Boy*, Pat Hickey walks us through the wilderness of transition from generation to generation, from culture to culture, breaking down the intellectual currency into street currency. He makes the metaphysical—physical…History is made personal and hysterical by Pat.

—**REV. CECIL L. "CHIP" MURRAY,** Minister Retired, First African Methodist Episcopal Church, Los Angeles

Tahoe Boy is a generous, extra "me" in the conversation, and honest and open friend with whom to compare notes…Pat Hickey's lively and engaging pen generously offers his half of the conversation…you hold a good book in your hands.

—**FRANK KAUFMANN, PH. D.**
Editor in Chief, *New World Encyclopedia*

From political caucus to pastoral cabin, Pat explores his life experiences, a journey that leads him back to his roots. *Tahoe Boy* is a truly enjoyable book. Pat's candor and comfortable style reveal the source of the commitment I saw when we served together in the Nevada Legislature.
—**LYNN HETTRICK,** Co-Speaker, Minority Leader Nevada Assembly

A globe-trotting journey of self-discovery that brings this son of the Sierra Nevada full-circle in his personal rite of passage...Pat Hickey writes with penetrating wit and wisdom. Buy this book, you will surely enjoy the experience.
—**GUY LOUIS ROCHA**
Nevada Public Historian and former State Archivist

Pat Hickey engagingly shares tales of his "balls to the walls life" and it is quite an adventure. You don't have to be an admirer of the Unification Church to appreciate his spiritual pilgrimage. His journeys from his Lake Tahoe childhood to stops hither and yon make this a tale worth reading
—**MARY HAUSCH,** Associate Professor of Journalism, U.N.L.V.

TAHOE BOY

A JOURNEY BACK HOME

PAT HICKEY

Dear Matt –
May you find
your own memories
too –
love,
Pat
, 5/28/2009

SEVEN LOCKS PRESS

Seven Locks Press
P.O. Box 25689
Santa Ana, CA 92799
(800) 354-5348

Individual sales: This book is available through most bookstores or can be ordered directly from Seven Locks Press at the address above.

Quantity Sales: Special discounts are available on quantity purchases by corporations, associations and others. For details, contact the "Special Sales Department" at the publisher's address above.

Cover & Interior Design Kira Fulks • www.kirafulks.com

www.sevenlockspublishing.com

Printed in the United States of America

Library of Congress Cataloging-in-Publication Data is available from the publisher

ISBN: 978-0-9822293-6-1 0-9822293-6-4

DEDICATION

To my Fathers,
for their love, their wisdom and their understanding.

FOREWORD

REV. CECIL L. "CHIP" MURRAY
Minister Retired, First African Methodist Episcopal Church,
Los Angeles, California

In *Tahoe Boy*, Pat Hickey walks us through the wilderness of transition from generation to generation, from culture to culture, breaking down the intellectual propriety into street currency. He makes the metaphysical physical. The beauty of this story is that it enables the reader to say, "Hey, that's me!" For instance, the cultural rebellion of the '60's alters *boarding school* to *bored in school,* and the snatched freedoms prevalent after sunset and out of sight. Thus the rebel mountain man obtains an independence that would have been impossible under the strict tutelage of parental supervision at home

Growing is growing up if you have rooted and supportive parents. They are there as you learn to ski, as you break a leg, learn to ride a bike, examine Catholic Church-going, wander in Desolation Wilderness and enter prep school in the age of rebellion. The book is an invitation to *ride with me* from the Depression of the 1920's to the recession of the present time, but these are only book marks for societal changes, culture classics, family values—transitions marked by movement from birth through the teens through progression to adulthood. History is made personal and hysterical by Pat.

The first year of college is goodbye to traditional values. The humor and the tragedy of the transition are spellbinding. Then Vietnam revolutionizes, particularly in the decided commitment to resist the draft. Then the Grand Canyon at age 21 says clearly, "The universal remedy for my generation [traveling] has lost its appeal." The challenge: "Not where to go; but what to become." The quest is ended, a new quest is begun. The teachings of Unification Church open the door to the answer: "Jesus, the man who became like God, was more compelling than Christ, the God who became like man." It is in Montana that Pat Hickey experiences a mystical revelation of the Second Coming of Christ, this time in the substance of Sun Myung Moon, so that at age 22 he becomes the first "man" to join the movement in Montana.

New York brings our writer to a meeting with Sun Myung Moon for the first time. This starts church missions that take him over the country and across continents, teaching the concept of the family as God's federation, marrying interracially and an arranged union made by the founder of the Unification movement.

He goes to the world and the world comes to him as the latter portions of his book deal with celebrities inclusive of such as Ronald Reagan, Jon Voight and Rush Limbaugh. The broad scope of varying interests of lives mentioned shows again the universality and scope of the author's concerns. Following work as a news editor, then as elected assemblyman in Nevada, convergence sets in, the pieces begin to fit. He enjoys politics, but notes with humor that politics have a tic that keeps you loose and free from demanding too much of human nature: "Being a political candidate isn't that different from being a religious missionary. Both require faith and thick skin."

His work ethic helps him get elected, but his family ethic does not allow a second term of office. He served well, daring to be out of step, showing that being out of step does not necessarily equate to being out of focus. Yes, "Someone else can fill my assembly seat. No one else can fill my shoes as a father."

His ultimate step is consolidation, making priority time for his four children and their mother, his love; building a cabin in Tahoe where the next generations may come in remembrance; passing on to us all that is Tahoe, but alerting us that somewhere over the rainbow there is a Tahoe in all of us. We find it and we find peace. At last the pieces fit.

Having worked with Pat Hickey for a score of years, having ministered to the hungry and the homeless together with our two faith systems, having bonded in social outreach, having studied the doctrines that guide our beliefs, having prayed together even though separated by circumstances and geography, I know him to be as a beloved son and I am ever proud of this Tahoe boy.

FOREWORD

Frank Kaufmann, Ph. D.

Editor in Chief, *The New World Encyclopedia*

History moves inexorably from "theirs" to "ours." This is happening to government, it will now happen to "economics," and it is happening to "history." *Tahoe Boy* participates on the avant garde of this positive and inevitable trend as we evolve to become more real, more true and more personally responsible as God's children.

The "truth" of a time, its phenomena and institutions, no longer come to us best from "authoritative" places bound in an individual or the elite. It increasingly comes to be discovered that "truth" is ours. It is the emerging and arising of tales told, of lives lived, and of personal responses to efforts by the divine infinite to touch and shape each of us, person by person.

We do want to know about our dramatic, historical era from the 1950's to the present. We do want to know all about household names like Richard Nixon, the Grateful Dead, Reverend Moon and Rush Limbaugh. But we no longer are satisfied only with theory, analysis and disengaged reflection. We want to know of our times, its people and its institutions and events as they relate to me. Our historical moment is one in which knowing is blossoming into one of relevance and life.

As I pursue my discovery of "truth," Tahoe Boy is a generous, extra "me" in the conversation, an honest and open friend with whom to compare notes.

What were the tumultuous decades of our era "really like"? What do they mean? And how do they inform our way forward in a constructive and hopeful way? One way to answer this question is to live in these words confessed by this "friend," Tahoe Boy, who tells of his own attempt to "be informed by these decades and move forward in a constructive and hopeful way."

Pat Hickey's lively and engaging pen generously offers his half of the conversation. How does his experience with the never-changing (teen romance, for example) compare to mine? How do his encounter and views on particular and unique realities (such as the Vietnam War, or Reverend Moon) compare to mine?

Answer back. As Tahoe Boy seeks the good, seek yours. These stories, these times, and this time are ours. We need one another. We need each voice and each story. These will allow us to hear, to learn, and humbly to bow down to every account of God's effort to touch our hearts, each of us one by one. Is there a Queens boy, a Chicago boy, an Idaho Girl speaking in the spaces between the words on these pages? If you hear the telling of your story in the silent spaces on these pages, if the good calls you and you hear yourself whispering of your embrace, you hold a good book in your hands.

TAHOE BOY

1

▼

Tahoe Boy

FINDING HAPPINESS IS DAMN HARD TO DO. Even growing up in a picture-perfect paradise like Lake Tahoe it wasn't easy. Friends of mine got lost looking for it in America's year-round blue playground. Many went elsewhere sojourning for their peace. I did it all before I came back home to find mine.

All life begins somewhere in time. Mine began in 1950, a good time in America. Good time because dads like mine had just come back from the war full of hope and pent-up ambitions ready to burst. Good times, because moms like Alynne were eager to give George the opportunity to be a full participant in the ensuing baby boom. Good place, Lake Tahoe. Because it is something like the "fairest picture the whole world affords," or so said Samuel Clemens before he began to joke a lot as Mark Twain.

My sister Sherrie is thirteen years older. Married at eighteen, she was gone before I got to know her. She has fond memories of caring for me. I have few of her. Without having brothers or sisters around, a wistful imagination was my soul companion. Imaginary playmates like Poncho were created to take the blame for boyhood misdeeds, but my parents weren't buying. A virtual only child, daydreams were of family that was large and warm. Like Eden before the fall, my Tahoe childhood went by mostly uninterrupted. Summers were spent by the Lake or throwing a baseball against a backyard log to imaginary big-league sluggers and fielding their response. Playing at friends' homes with bigger families and kid noises that welcomed made me wish for a future of the same.

Ski Run home
Winter of 1952

As a teenager I wondered if hometown and family were all there'd ever be. Figuring that getting to where I wanted to go involved getting away from where I came, I spent my days dreaming about going away. But as any teenager will tell you, you can't make it to the future without going through the present. And the ever-present for any young person are his parents and their world. They, of course, had family and a past as well.

Enterprising Cuss

MY PATERNAL GRANDFATHER, Pat Hickey, was a potato-famine Irishman who arrived in Carson City in 1877 with his immigrant family of nine. After growing up, Pat took a local girl, Adeline Higsan, from the Carson Valley as his wife. As the oldest boy, he inherited the 400-acre homesteaded Hickey Ranch near Nevada's disputed first Western settlement, Genoa, on the East Side of the Sierra Nevada Range. There in 1913 in the family farm house on Mottsville Lane, my father, George, was born.

From all accounts, Grandpa Pat was an enterprising cuss. Not foolish enough to remain a dirt-poor Irish farmer; neither was he wise enough to become a land-rich American rancher. Instead, Pat harvested ice out of brother-in-law Wallace Park's frozen pond. You've seen it on television. It's the one NBA legend Charles Barkley slices his tee shots into every summer during the Edgewood Tahoe Celebrity Golf Classic. That water hazard holds the distinction of being the only place I know of that both Sir Charles and my grandfather cursed at incessantly. Another tale of the family's land has Mark Twain penning parts of *Roughing It* at Edgewood, or Friday's Station, as it was known then. It served as a Pony Express stop for the likes of Snowshoe Thompson and his beleaguered mail carriers, as well as a place for Pat to get a back door plate of Irish stew from sister, Maggie Park.

No one can say for sure that Eugene O'Neill used my grandfather as his model for the 1939 "Hickey" of *The Iceman Cometh* fame, but he did resemble the play's central character in two important ways. Pat loved to talk and he loved to drink; not necessarily in that order. As fate would have it, gambling was legalized in Nevada in 1931. Notice I didn't say it actually began in the Silver State that year. Prohibition dried up by 1933, but the Anti-Saloon League never had much of a chance in Nevada anyway. And if you don't see the connection between alcohol and wagering, then I'd ask you to look again.

Old Pat must have heard what Mark Twain reputedly joked about how Nevadans will fight over water but give you whiskey for free. Visit any Vegas casino and introduce yourself to a mechanized one-armed bandit, and a pretty young thing with impressive cleavage will appear offering a complimentary adult beverage to loosen you and your pocketbook up. The second part of Twain's Western wisdom also still holds. Try building a poker parlor in Nevada, and see which is harder–getting a liquor license or finding a well deep enough to sustain it.

Even without much formal education, Pat understood the correlation between gambling and ice. To that end, his frozen solids found their way into the drinks that card sharks and dice-rollers drank in the early days of Nevada's second legalized vice. Don't misunderstand, my short iceman grandfather serviced the common man as well. First by buggy and then by Ford, he went up and down lakeside staircases delivering the one thing that would keep folks' food fresh. Unfortunately, most of Pat's regular customers were kind enough to keep a bottle of Irish whiskey under the sink. That, combined with his natural inclination to gab, presented the Hickey Ice Company with a major challenge. My grandfather solved the problem by bringing on board the buggy the first designated driver in recorded Nevada history to help complete his daily deliveries before they melted.

Property bordering the California state line on Tahoe's South Shore would one day become priceless and worth squabbling over as Wallace Park's descendants, and my cousins, would later discover. Then, it was merely a swollen dirt highway with wooden roadhouses designed for wealthy San Franciscans to stop and contribute the fruits of their commerce to Nevada casino coffers; a tradition that still thrives in Stateline. Unlike today in parts of Tahoe where it's said billionaires have driven the millionaires away, lakefront property could be purchased cheaply in the early twentieth century, even by an immigrant iceman with a few questionable habits.

Pat Hickey acquired 40 acres of lakefront meadowland south of Marla Bay on Nevada's eastern shore of the Lake. There he built a cabin the family stayed in during the summer months. He contracted with an orange grower from Southern California and operated a fruit stand along the highway to serve vacationing patrons as they passed by in their open-air Model T's. In those days, the Great Depression stuck its squalid hand in most pocketbooks. My grandfather's was no exception. Out of necessity he sold the land that would have made his descendants rich. More than money, he lost a Tahoe treasure that no amount of real estate dividends could ever replace.

Tommy Hilfiger's co-founder now owns the property called Tranquility Estate. The last time I checked, they were selling it for $100 million. Not having the $99.9 million it would take to reclaim the property on behalf of Pat's honor or my descendants' trust fund, I wish them well. Given the success of their designer label sales, I doubt they'll ever need to open an orange stand to keep it afloat.

While old Pat lost the cabin, he held on to the ice business long enough to give it to my father in 1945 when he returned from hiding from the Japanese in Burma. One year later Pat was laid to rest. I never got to meet my grandfather. But I am now, conjuring up these tales about him. I hope he found his peace. I suspect he's lounging with a glass of Irish whiskey in a sweet-tranquility estate of his own making, curious about the written way I'm trying to connect.

3

Too Much Testosterone
and Too Few Social Outlets

IN THE INTEREST OF AVOIDING a family feud upstairs, let me tell you about my mother's family. While the noble pilgrims landed earlier in Plymouth, my mother's ancestor Samuel Newell came from Ireland to America in 1730 and made his way to the Shenandoah Valley. He came in search not of some noble notion of religious freedom –but for farmland.

My grandfather Cleveland Newell's clan eventually migrated to Red Lodge, Montana. Cleve was born there in 1884. With his eight brothers and sisters, he grew up on the Western frontier. Unlike Pat, there were actually a few unflattering facts written about him. Mostly trivial things like, "full of hell," "Mama was not too thrilled at having one of those Newell boys for a son-in-law," or "Cleve made a disrespectful remark about the ancestry of old Tuck." Not a bad fellow, he was just a young man growing up on the desolate edge of Yellowstone, with too much testosterone and too few social outlets.

By all accounts, Cleve was the character of the family. His brother

Joe said of him, "Damned guy was always stirring up something before we older boys had to bale him out." Between the chuckle and the grin you never got the impression that Joe was unhappy about the fact. Cleve's sister-in-law, Susan Carr Newell, tells the following stories: "Cleve started courting the new teacher in Roberts, a Miss Josephine Thompson. Things were going right well, and he finally asked her to marry him. But she made it clear: the wedding would be after he was off probation and behaved himself for a whole year!"

Josie, my grandmother, was a pretty woman; trim and a no-nonsense kind of a lady. Josie took on a real job when she married Cleve. She not only got Cleve but got his dad too. She had her hands full with those two men. Old John loved to tease and Cleve was no slouch about it either. One day Josie was on her knees frying meat over the stove. John came by and said something to her, and the next thing you knew, she dumped the beef in the fire and took after him with a skillet. The only thing that saved his life that he was able to outrun her in that long skirt. She made him confess his sin before he got back into camp. Cleve just laughed and commented to his father, Dad–you should know better than to rile the cook."

In 1920 Cleve and Josie brought their three daughters by train from Montana to California. My mother, Alynne, was three years old when the trip was made. Their grandfather pampered the girls with apples and oranges bought along the way. After a few moves around the Golden State, they settled in Chico where they could grow their own. There, in that now sleepy college town, memories of my grandparents begin and end. I remember afternoon baseball on the radio, the brown leather chair and his always-available lap. I remember her backyard hammock near the summer house and the stars of August she'd get me to count before I became a goner. I remember the black bumble bee in her backyard of green and white clovers and the yellow butter she lovingly applied to its purple sting. I remember his linguistic skills! A serious role model for Samuel L. Jackson in *Pulp Fiction*, Cleveland Newell could quote the Bible and cuss with equal lucidity. It remains only a rumor that he once shot someone back in Montana while doing both.

My grandparents died within a year of each other. Together in this life, they moved on in pursuit of a shared happiness in the next. More was written and more could be said. But that's their story and this is mine. Still, for anyone who goes digging up the past with an eye to the future—parts of the puzzle are embedded deep in family. If it's true that we are all the fruit of someone, it was good to have tasted the sweet residue of theirs.

4

▼

Little Was Said About the Lot That Was Done

CHILDHOOD MEMORIES OF MY FATHER are more bittersweet. Having grown up in Gardnerville and surviving the down days of the American Depression, Dad was drafted in 1941. After boot camp he was shipped off to a place he'd never heard of before. Passing through Bombay and Calcutta to get there, my father witnessed deprivation that would haunt him for the rest of his life. Hard times in rural Nevada paled in comparison to the endless sea of poor he found tugging on his G.I. fatigues as he crossed the Indian Subcontinent. To this day, a proposed visit to a restaurant with curry on the menu will get you a cantankerous stare and a quick cuisine change.

My father's Army orders were to keep the Burma Railroad running. The Japanese had contrary orders. Master Sergeant Hickey and the Chinese coolies working for him would rebuild the tracks one day, and dive-bombing Zeroes would obliterate them the next. For his time spent hiding in caves along the Burma Highway, he came home with a Bronze Star. But like most from a great generation, little was said about the lot that was done.

The regularity of the bombing runs actually improved Japanese-American relations, at least out in the middle of the Burmese nowhere. By the time 1945 rolled around, my father and his Japanese counterparts were secretly trading supplies at a nearby riverbank convinced that, whatever in the world was going on between Tokyo and Washington, it had little bearing on them. That seemingly insignificant act of personal East-West détente may have foreshadowed a thawing in his parochial Yankee worldview that would one day help him accept

My Father, George
Burma, 1942

my arranged marriage to an Asian woman. But long before that peace accord was struck, the groundwork for a war between our generations was being laid.

By the time my father got back from the war, the ice business was his. So were other entrepreneurial opportunities befitting a World War II veteran with plenty of catching up to do. With the combat pay he'd earned, George added a heating oil company to his resume. Combined with the ice company, my Dad was fond of saying that the family "kept folks warm in the winter and cool in the summer." One of his regular oil customers was Ty Cobb, the baseball Hall of Famer. Cobb retired near Logan's Shoal on the East Side of the Lake. The press said old Ty was mean-spirited to a fault. Being a kid, I never saw that side of him. I suppose he was nicer to me than the poor shortstops he once slid into. He gave me a Louisville Slugger I keep in my office.

As if two fledgling enterprises weren't enough, my father agreed to take on the role of local Bijou Postmaster. Thoroughly overworked, at least he stayed busy enough to avoid any post-war syndromes. Next, seeing what appeared to be an under-utilized young man, an official from the U.S. Forest Service approached him about starting a local garbage company. Until then, resident black bears had been disposing of humans' waste in the basin, and apparently they were hibernating the winter day my father was propositioned. Once again, ambition won out over his mental day timer, and George Hickey was now South Lake Tahoe's founding CEO of garbage collection.

The Forest Service was even kind enough to offer a dump site off the dirt road, Pioneer Trail. Sixty years later, government agencies apparently regret that environmentally mistaken move. The canyon they provided Dad for dumping old sofas and coffee grounds into happened to also contain Trout Creek that found its way into the pristine lake below. An attorney representing the large conglomerate that now owns the Tahoe Basin's million-dollar waste-management company recently bumped into my 96-year-old father at a family reunion at the J.T. Saloon in Gardnerville. He told my dad his name came up in a recent Environmental Protection Agency deposition. Mulling the implications while finishing their brandies, both men agreed that by the time the government got around to making it into something federal like a Superfund site, my father would be pushing up daises anyway. Besides, as my father pointed out, it was Smokey that came up with the bright idea for the dump in the first place.

The Hickey Garbage Company did provide certain ecological benefits to the local habitat. Having garbage at his disposal, my father got the inspiration for starting another enterprise: a hog business.

After all, the dump's contents provided pigs with enough grist for their voracious appetites. Hearing of my Dad's dilemma, a butcher in Carson City offered to beat the bears to the punch and surgically prepare the pork for human consumption. The food chain was further linked by the neighborhood black bears who viewed the addition of pigs to their environment as an opportunity to feast on raw bacon. This in turn provided another species, the Homo sapiens night watchman, with the task of keeping the bears at bay with his trusted Winchester. No species above or below the human level ever tried to eat the constantly sobering-up guard, but I remember my mother having to bring a weekly supply of groceries and beer to keep him posted at the shack. To my knowledge, no one ever approached my dad about a bear-rug business. I'm sure he would have leaped at the chance.

5

Wood Bats and Dress Shoes Were Not a Stylish Match

AS DESCRIBED, MY FATHER WORKED himself to the bone. In turn, he did his best to pass along the family legacy to me. I was introduced to the pleasure of labor during the summer of 1959 when I was nine. My father lured me into the twenty-nine degree ice house downstairs with the logic that it was 109 degrees hotter outside in the shade. My solution to the heat would have been to join my friends at the beach. You can guess whose logic won out. That summer officially began a career as an ice-cube bagger. My friends got their tans. I practically got frostbite.

There in the freezer, decades before meeting my first Oriental sage, I learned the principle of *yin and yang* and polar opposites. By going from hot to cold and in and out of that God damn ice house, I became acquainted with the Buddhist Wheel of Becoming, or suffering as it's more commonly known. Unfortunately, it was without the benefit of enlightenment. At the time, it seemed only my father was being blessed and profiting from my devotion. Forced labor in the summertime eliminated most picnics at the beach. However, in some pre-pubescent way, it made me proud to be working for the family business.

My father, like his father before him, delivered Hickey ice to the nearby Stateline casinos. When their ice machines broke down on a busy Saturday night, they would call George at home in the middle of the night. My mother, feeling for Dad's bad back, would wake me up and send me downstairs and help him load the truck. Most nights I'd pretend to sleep through her attempts. But on the times I parked my attitude and descended into the nighttime cold below, I was rewarded with the satisfaction of being a partner in the family tradition of overwork. Meritorious late-night service did have its benefits. An early morning French toast breakfast usually followed unloading the fifty-pound bags of cubes that kept Whiskey on the Rocks a viable option for Harrah's and Harvey's.

My dad made what time he could for me. Among the things he did was to coach Little League and Babe Ruth baseball. I was automatically drafted onto his teams, which had its pros and cons. The fun part was behaving like a wisecracking son of a coach in front of my adolescent teammates. The bad part was not getting away with acting like the jerk that I was, especially when the coach was in the dugout. To his credit, he was not above benching me.

Paul Marsh was another story. Our other pitcher, he had the body of the young Bambino and the appetite to go with it. He would successfully hit my dad up for a hot dog before and after every game. I think my Father saw potential in Paul and his tube steak fetish. Marsh later became a butcher at Safeway at the South Shore.

I wasn't the only member of our Babe Ruth team that found humor in my Dad's coaching style. Upon being selected as one of our All Star coaches, he decided to upgrade his wardrobe for the occasion. Not having any baseball cleats in his coaching closet, my father wore his black wing tip shoes normally reserved for weddings and funerals. *Queer Eye for the Straight Guy* was still a long time away, but we thirteen-year-old knuckleheads knew ridiculous when we saw it. Wood bats and dress shoes were not a stylish match. Neither was my pitching, and we got slaughtered by Susanville in that year's short-lived postseason.

6

Heavenly Valley and Friday the 13th

IF YOU GREW UP IN HAWAII, you learned to surf. At Lake Tahoe, you learned to ski. And if your home happened to be on Ski Run Boulevard, it was only a short climb to Heavenly Valley. *Heavenly,* as it's now known, opened its main chairlift in 1955, the year I learned to ski. Stein Erickson, the world's prettiest alpine skier and recent Olympic gold medalist, opened his first ski school at *Heavenly* and taught me how to ski. It didn't take long for this five year-old to become a Stein impersonator.

It was Friday, February 13, 1958, and a huge load of "Sierra cement" (as Tahoe's wet snow is called) had dumped on the slopes the night before. To my delight, school officials cancelled classes. I don't recall my mother being overly superstitious, but she was overly a mother. Before leaving for the slopes, she reminded me that going skiing on Friday the 13th wasn't a good idea. It wouldn't be the first parental warning that went unheeded, or the last not-so-smart thing I'd ever do.

Back then, Heavenly Valley wasn't the destination resort that it is today. It did, and still does, have one of sport's most revered mogul runs. Straight down the face of the mountain, it's called the Gun Barrel. Standing at the top of its 1,600-foot vertical drop, it looks like you're peering down the barrel of a Dirty Harry peacemaker. It's a formidable ski run even for an Olympian. Given the day's road conditions and my home's close proximity to the lifts, a lone ski patrolman – and yours truly – were the only two fools on the hill that ill-fated afternoon.

Somewhere it's written about American ingenuity and government regulation. The two don't necessarily go together. In the case of the safety binding, I wish they had. The following year safety bindings would be required on all American skis. In 1958 they were not. I had the bad fortune of having ancient bear-trap bindings strapped to my boards. Like the name, once you're clamped into to a bear-trap binding, there's no getting out.

Unbeknownst to me, my mother was seeing something I wished she hadn't. The minute I fell I knew my leg was broken. There I was, at eight years old, on the steepest part of the Gun Barrel with my left ski sticking like an arrow through the back of the mogul. My Mom, watching from the lower lodge's sundeck, got lift operators to radio my Red Cross savior. He arrived in time to release me from the clutches of the bear trap and place my skis in the traditional "X marks the accident," confirming my mother's fears and validating her warning. With tears flowing she reminded me of both as the ski patrol toboggan rode past her on its way to the ambulance. When you give yourself the gift of a spiral fracture to the tibia, your body at least does you a favor. It sends you into shock, suspending the pain – at least until the doctor sets the break.

Three months in a plaster cast was a mixed blessing. It meant missing school and having a pretty young tutor who helped with my homework. It also meant having an itchy leg that I couldn't get at except with a Tonka toy angled through a hole I bored in the cast through my best friend's name. Later, my injury provided me with an excuse for not yet knowing how to ride a bike.

7

Like God—
She Was Always Around

BY THE NEXT SUMMER, my friends had all discovered that riding a bicycle is a boy's first taste of freedom. With two wheels, you can go to games by yourself, spy on a new-girl-in-school's house, or leave home on a stealth mission to the candy store after you've pilfered enough quarters from your parents' dresser. It didn't go unnoticed that my friends tasted that first freedom in advance of me. And while the previous winter's accident gave me an excuse for not joining their escapades, it was clear that it was also keeping me out of a lot of their fun. Determined to come back from the leg break and my reservations about straddling air on a Schwinn, I set out to exercise the ghost of the two-wheeler and gain my balance on a bike. Or die trying. The sheet metal well cover in the backyard made for a good launching pad and propelled me wobbling forward before each crash.

Like God, my mother was invisible but always around. Through the bathroom window she watched with a mixture of pity and pride as I bruised both ego and elbows. It was a long summer day before I met with success. My mother later reported that in the course of learning to ride that damn bike, she noticed I'd inherited one of the principal characteristics of her father, Cleve. No, I wasn't quoting Psalms about some veritable valley of death. Instead, I was spewing out cuss words she'd only heard her father ever use.

My Mother, Alynne
1943

Not to be outdone, my father also had me dialed in. One day my folks and I visited the George Waite family at their home in Stateline. Tired of grownup chatter and tossing the usual snowballs at the nearby Postmaster's door; George Jr. and I snuck away from the purview of our parents and headed on our bikes across the horse stables meadow to nearby Cecil's Market. Cecil's was the first store at the South Shore. My father had bagged groceries there as a kid

The new manager was fairly undistinguished, but his twelve-year-old daughter was a whole different story. There's something about a new girl in school. The allure of the unknown, verses the cooties of the known, makes for a temporary mystique. We were about to learn she was untouchable. She would soon see we were from a lower caste.

Lurking across the street, hoping to get a glimpse through an upstairs bedroom window, Georgie and I never saw my father coming. He'd snuck across the meadow and come up behind us. I don't know which was worse—the horrors of him crying and chasing me all the way back home, or the impending embarrassment the next day at school. I'll never forget the anguished look on my dad's face that

Heavenly Valley, 1956

night. Not until I became a father did I fully appreciate that primal urge to protect. Strangely, that dark night's act of parental desperation has stayed with me for forty-nine years as a defining moment in my father's heritage of love.

Another way he showed his love was to always be at the finish gate of my ski races. Win, loose, or blizzard—I could count on him being there at the bottom of the hill. The funny thing was, the end of a race course was not always at the base of the resort. His iceman's bad back prevented him from skiing. So he'd walk all the way up and all the way back down in the deep snow. His presence never helped me win or loose a race. But seeing him there shivering in blowing storms made an impression I didn't fully appreciate until I had two sons of my own.

The winter after my broken leg, the family took a ski trip to Aspen. We went by train through the Nevada desert, by Utah canyons and alongside Colorado Rockies, before arriving at the maze of train tracks they call Grand Junction. We stayed at the Hotel Jerome, an Aspen landmark. Wealthy Texans holidayed in Aspen in those days, and made sure to tell everyone about being both Texan and wealthy.

Besides skiing down venerable Aspen Mountain, I had the good fortune of meeting U.S. Olympic legend Buddy Werner at the town's oldest establishment, the Red Onion. With my parents' prodding, I shuffled nervously over to his party's table with napkin and pen in hand. He gladly gave me his best wishes and boyish grin. It was a proud day in my young life. Sadly, Buddy's life ended soon after at the tender age of 28. He was killed in a Swiss skiing accident making a documentary on the life he loved. No one more epitomized American youth and idealism than Buddy Werner. Having met him, I thought you should know that. The '60's missed having Buddy around.

We also managed to miss the train back to Reno. I'd sprained my ankle the day before and when we got to the station at Grand Junction I was on crutches and the train wasn't waiting. My parents ran after the caboose in hopes of getting the conductor to pull the stop. I limped behind, slightly discouraged, when I heard my father yell, "Just leave him!" The Tahoe Zephyr ended up leaving all three of us in its wake. My father then paid a taxi driver a bizarre amount of money to break the land speed record and get us in true Great Race style ahead of the train and to the next stop, which he eventually did.

When we finally boarded, my parents headed straight for the bar. I overheard the conductor say, "If only they had called, we would have waited." If only for an earlier invention of the cell phone, my father would have saved the dough he spent on our wild ride and the extra booze he needed in the club car to recover from it. Anyway, I'm glad we didn't have that bothersome digital luxury back then. It would have eliminated a melodrama worth remembering. Just as the constant cell-phone companions we carry with us today get in the way of so much that is ordinary and human.

I always thought that if I ever wrote something, I'd include a piece about another skier who died before his time. His name was Johnny Brown. From Reno, Johnny was a cherub-like blond boy from the rival *Falcons*. We'd met up occasionally on slalom courses. He, too, was buried in a premature white grave by a solitary avalanche in the Shutes on the back side of the aptly named Slide Mountain. Long before extreme skiing became a craze, Johnny took off for one last run in search of the pleasure of fresh powder. I do hope I meet Johnny again someday—on a celestial hill of his choosing.

If the Almighty is indeed beyond space and time, powder skiing is akin to the divine. Our band of *Blue Angels* would go anywhere in search of it. Off the skied-out marked runs, our racing team made trails of our own. The original copywriters of "Dead Man's Grade," one of our secret runs spiraled down the back side of Heavenly through untouched snow inside of unknown gulches. Getting there required three times as much hiking as it did to ski down. But fresh powder was always worth the price of the aching thighs it took to find it.

It was even better when we introduced a new devotee to our path. Alan Hagerty was the downhill specialist of our team, and became our first initiate. Because he was more than a little overweight, it was side-splittingly stupid watching him struggle to ascend to the heights of our secret run. It also helped that Alan's dad was our elementary school P.E. teacher. The sins of a father could be paid for by the son. Seeing Hagerty huff and puff up those slopes gave us a convoluted sense of revenge for all the laps his old man made us run.

8

UFO's in Desolation Valley

GROWING UP AT THE LAKE, there were plenty of places in nature to play tricks on your friends. Desolation Wilderness Area, west of the Lake, was a favorite. Backpacking in for the weekend, we'd bring a buddy up its granite trails to fish at one of the high Sierra lakes. The table would then be set for our adolescent scam. While sitting around the campfire before nightfall, we'd tell the prospective sap of the recent sightings of flying objects above the basin's towering peaks. And sure enough, once the sun set, strange lights would appear and dance around the sky above us as we peeked out from inside our flannel sleeping bags. The ruse worked on gullible young guys because at that age you're so in the dark about reality, you'll easily believe in the extraterrestrial. In fact, the apparent UFOs were spotlights from our old friends the South Shore casinos announcing that Frank Sinatra would be singing in the showroom that night. Our ploy worked because the desire to believe in something is almost always stronger than the reasons not to.

One night in Desolation Valley, I paid for my shenanigans. Waking up the next morning, there was a solid layer of mosquito bites in rows across my forehead. I gave up trying to count them because they'd melded into one continuous itchy bump. God apparently judged me for lying about the UFO's by sending a fleet of minuscule proboscidate devils to extract payment in blood for my misdeeds.

9

Catholic School

As FOR GOD'S JUDGMENTS, at that point in my life I was more or less in the Tom Sawyer School of Theology. Twain's Tom, who questioned Aunt Polly about the efficacy of regular church attendance, was told that if he didn't go on Sundays, he'd end up in Hell. Asking about the attributes of life in Heaven, Tom was told it would be like the church service he was regularly avoiding—a lot of hymn singing and damnation talk. Tom told his aunt he'd prefer to enjoy life in the warmer place with Huck, Becky Thatcher and Old Joe. At twelve, my thinking resembled that notion. Even now, I'd prefer to spend an eternity with someone like Tom and my mostly apostate friends. Sign me up for that Sawyer jamboree—even if it's a little hot where he resides.

Besides, not all my friends were welcome at church. In the fifth grade, our local Catholic parish, St. Theresa's, opened an elementary school on the South Shore. Thinking as parents do today, that a parochial education is superior to a secular one, my friend Bobby Maro's non-religious parents sent him to school there along with good Catholic boys like me. Obligated to attend the school's Mass on Fridays with the rest of us true believers, Bobby got in line the first Friday to receive the Holy Eucharist from Father Grace. He appeared appropriately pious; or at least until Sister Mary David grabbed him by the nape of the neck. Not having had his sins forgiven by the sacrament of Baptism, Bobby was not about to receive his First Communion outside of Canon Law.

Running into Bobby at a high-school reunion some 38 years later, I asked him if he'd ever stepped foot in a church again after that childhood incident. He said no. Vatican II would convene in a couple of years and Catholics would become more ecumenical like John XXIII. Then, the Church was the one apostolic faith, and souls like Bobby Maro weren't always welcome in the sanctuary.

The one place that welcomes all souls is a casino. No denominational litmus test required to enter. Just bring enough denominations of the green stuff—and you're in. Going to frequent dinner shows with my parents at Harrah's South Shore Room, we saw performers in their heyday. Headliners like Wayne Newton, Red Skelton and Bill Cosby entertained our threesome. How can anybody forget Bill Cosby as Fat Albert? Cosby seemed so fun-loving on stage. The different look I observed on his countenance at a crap table after his performance may have been because Harrah's was recouping his paycheck. I heard through a friend's father who was a casino pit boss that Cosby was a notorious gambler. And given that he still performs around the Lake some forty-five years later, I'm guessing he may still be involved in paying somebody back.

Cosby has become cranky in his old age, not liking the way inner city kids talk and all. I hope he gets his happy back before he passes on. I think comedian Red Skelton never lost his; or any of his money at the gaming tables. Red was a good Catholic and always said "God

Bless" and truly meant it at the end of his nightly pantomimes. Even Bob Maro would have felt welcome at one of Red's benedictions. Don't get me wrong, I'm not anti-Vatican. Sister Mary David would never stand for that. Then again, she's not a nun anymore; and I'm not much of a Catholic.

I was the first altar boy chosen from the new class at St. Theresa's to serve Mass for Father Grace. His Irish brogue and the Latin liturgy always made it difficult to decipher the exact moment for ringing the bells and pouring the Holy Water. It was even harder when Father Henry, the parish's Italian priest, was saying Mass. Father Henry was a sociable old soul with a gruff Sicilian accent. When an altar boy got caught napping in the kneeling position and missed a chime, Father Henry would stop and scold him in front of the whole congregation. Not part of the traditional liturgy; it at least let churchgoers know they weren't the only sinners in attendance that Sunday.

One of Father Henry's most infamous priestly pronouncements came on a day I was serving Mass. Having forgotten to pour the red substance from a vine to reenact, in an unbloody manner, Jesus' bloody sacrifice on the Cross, Father Henry called for "MORE WINE" in his loud guttural drawl that had the whole church laughing in the pews. Heck, Jesus probably got a kick out of it as well. After all, he'd been listening to the Church hierarchy speaking to God in Italian for the past 2,000 years and probably heard a lot of requests for more wine, permission to marry and better stipends.

Confirmation is an important milestone in the life of a young Catholic. It's the Church's sacramental rite of passage affirming the acceptance of Baptism. Since you are two weeks old when you get your watery induction into the Roman flock, it's probably a good idea to get a soul to buy into the appointment about twelve years later. Before getting my forehead anointed by the Bishop, I was pre-selected by

Father Grace to answer a question about the doctrines of the Church. Having answered the first one correctly and my classmates being either too shy or too sleepy to respond to the second, the Bishop turned again to me in the hopes that at least one young Tahoe believer had been studying his Catechism before being confirmed in his faith. I got lucky again. I later heard from my parents there were whispers among the faithful that I might someday discover a vocation as a priest. That wasn't going to happen. I had too many questions and too much of an attraction to girls for me to ever last in a seminary.

I had a ton of questions. Like why, if you were a Catholic and your original sin had been removed by Baptism and you then married a Catholic spouse whose original sin had also been forgiven, wouldn't children of such a marriage be born without original sin? No one had an answer for that one. I concluded the Church didn't want to get out of the salvation business by making one of its Sacraments obsolete.

That kind of thinking would one day get me into trouble in late night rap sessions with the Christian Brothers at boarding school. For the time being, I remained in the good graces of Father Grace. Demonstrating his willingness to forgive beyond the Confessional, Father would always consider me a good lad. Even after he learned that I was in the clutches of Reverend Moon, he told my parents, "Once a Catholic, always a Catholic." The old Irish cleric is now retired and plays a lot of free golf at Edgewood, a gift the family gave to him for being such a kindly shepherd.

10

Boarding School

IN 1964, I WENT AWAY TO BOARDING SCHOOL at St. Mary's College High School in Berkeley. A number of Tahoe parents sent their first-born males there to save them from the scourge of public education. It was too early for parents to know that sacrilegious singers like Madonna were a product of a Catholic high school, and not the moral panacea they presumed. The school was all-boys, all the time; which meant there was constant thought about imaginary girls.

Berkeley back then was in the early pangs of a cultural revolution that would forever change America. Cal students could be seen wearing bushy beards usually reserved for grizzled old miners and vagrants where I came from. Odder yet, the bearded U.C. Berkeley boys rode bicycles around campus. Strange because the dream of every fourteen-year-old I knew was to have traded in his two-wheeler for a 57 Chevy at least by your junior year in high school. To still be peddling around town in college appeared semi-retarded to my friends and me. So much so, we didn't think anybody would mind if we liberated a few of the unlocked two-wheelers for a trek around the Berkeley Hills. Upon finishing our joy ride we were met by campus police who didn't buy into the '60's notion that private property was passé. Given that we were first-time juvenile offenders, and Brother Richard's assurances to St. Mary's grad Chief Gorman that he was a firm believer in corporal punishment, we were dispatched back to the dorm record-free where a public flogging awaited us.

The Christian Brothers are well known for their brandy. Less known for their wisdom, the Prefects of Resident Students served as surrogate parents to a bunch of boys who had just finished reading *Catcher in the Rye* and *Lord of the Flies*, and felt like the alienated victims of both. Late-night rap sessions were necessary to keep peace among the warring tribes of freshman, sophomores, juniors and seniors living together on one floor. Never allowable in today's era of Surgeon General's warnings and tobacco companies' pretensions against teenage smoking, St. Joseph's Hall had a smoking lounge open to each and every aspiring James Dean who could squeeze in. Doors opened when we finished mandatory study hall, and soon there appeared 45 guys sucking on nicotine receptors in a fog thicker than the nearby San Francisco Bay. Maybe it was a ploy to get us not to smoke. At any rate, by sanctioning the lounge, it relieved the Brothers from the nightly duty of patrolling the bushes for puff-crazed offenders. Whatever the case, it was cool to be there in the lounge, regardless of how hot and bothersome it was–which is how we generally felt about being in a prep school.

Most weekends we'd figure out whose parents were out of town and hitch a ride to raid their vulnerable fridge and wet bar. As in life, getting there was half the horror. Being picked up by drunks, perverts and escapees from mental hospitals was commonplace. Coming back late to the dorm on Sunday night was routine until public punishments by Brother Richard made tardiness no longer an option.

First Communion With Father Grace and Greg Keller.
(I am the boy standing second from the right in the second row
with Greg to my right)

My childhood best friend Greg Keller also went to St. Mary's. We'd both grown up at the Lake and had been through a lot together before going away to boarding school. He once refused to fight me after I drew a line in the front lawn, questioning his loyalty as a friend. I remained mum and withstood his mother's interrogation the time he ran away to Hawaii for a week with Marion Babich. Later we'd be battle-tested from Saturday-night brawls at South Shore's American Legion Hall where "mountain men" mixed it up regularly with "flatlanders" on Friday and Saturday nights. All was preparation for our biggest test of the code.

We'd come home for the weekend from Berkeley to stock up on home cooking and exaggerated tales to take back to the guys in the dorm. Too cool to still ride bikes and too young yet to drive, walking was all that was available. That particular autumn night, as was always the case, there was no place to go. We decided instead to just hang out. This by the way is as bad an adolescent plan as you can draw up. Wandering around after dark for two 14 year-old males is a sure invitation for the Devil to get involved in an idle teenage mind.

For some reason Greg remembered that his next-door neighbor kept a key to the old pickup parked on the street under its left floorboard. Inspired by either boredom or the demonic, we decided to embark on another joy ride. Like the previous bicycle caper, we had every intention of bringing Fred's truck back when we finished with it. We took the decrepit Dodge up an old dirt road around Heavenly Valley. I was the driver because I'd supposedly learned to drive a stick shift backing up my father's truck to the loading dock at the ice house. Going up a steep section of the rocky grade, *Old Betsy* fell out of gear. Time stood still as Greg and I turned and looked at each other in our best Alfred E. Newman impressions–before jumping out of the truck before it crashed. In what seemed like double slow motion, the pickup rolled back down the hill, rear-ended a bank to the right, and drove slowly by itself off the side of the hill to the left. Unlike a *Dukes of Hazzard* rerun, the crash didn't result in an explosion; but then again, we didn't stick around long enough to see what damage we'd done.

Greg recently told me that night's incident changed his life. Instead of becoming a carjacker, he went on to be a U.S. Forest Service hotshot, a career every bit as dangerous but hardly as illegal. Speaking of talking about the incident, Greg and I ran all the way back to our respective homes and never said a word about it until at least a month later in a quiet corner of the dorm. We did learn that old Fred retrieved his truck, mostly undamaged. And unless the statute of limitations has not run out after 44 years, I think Keller and I are finally in the clear. We won't be though if Sister Mary David ever reads this. Though she's not a nun anymore, we both are certain she's still watching us.

Upon hearing this for the first time, my mother is probably turning over in her urn. Then again, there was enough she learned about me during her actual time on earth to result in an eternity of Rosaries recited in the next realm.

Lest you think the curriculum at St. Mary's was nothing more than a primer for grand auto theft, let me emphatically say–that for most, it wasn't. There were extraordinarily gifted teachers who cared deeply for the education of young Catholic men's hearts and minds. Some even succeeded in getting through to us. Most did not.

Two instructors come to mind, neither of them men of the cloth. Mr. Paul Conny was our English Teacher. He was white and always wore Brooks Brothers suits. Mr. Conny sported a five o'clock shadow by noon, and would sweat profusely whenever spitballs hit his blackboard exceeding three inches in diameter. The other, Mr. Ron Barrett, taught us U.S. history. He was black, carried himself like a Marine, added Mr. before every student's name, and commanded the rapt attention of even the worst petty criminals among us.

Mr. Conny's heart bled so much it hemorrhaged. He would plead, cajole and finally cry when our classroom pranks brought him to the breaking point. His sincerity dripped like his sweat. The inmates were in control and he knew it. Sensitivity and innate goodness were no match for teenage machismo and guile. Mr. Conny wore his heart on his sleeves, but never rolled them up to show us the toughness we needed. I rather hope he became a girls' school teacher. At least they don't throw spit wads.

"Bad Ass" Barrett was just that. He treated the smart, the dumb and every pretender in between–each the same. Same tone of respect, same squinty suspicion and same high expectation of each. If you didn't know a history fact, Mr. Barrett expected you would by the next time he called on you; and you did. Not till the last day of class did B.A. Barrett let down his guard. By then you'd made it through his scholar's gauntlet and he'd let you in on the fact that he wasn't such a bad guy after all. I hope he became a principal. Kids deserve a bad ass and a good man like him.

Sending your child off to a boarding school might be more risky than you think. Many parents assume they're doing a wise thing by enrolling their child in a prestigious prep school. Brother Mel, now President of St. Mary's College in Moraga, sent home a summer letter after my freshman year, thanking families for making boarding "a worthy experience in joyful and cooperative family living." The problem was with his premise. Besides making boarding school sound like a Chinese communal experiment, is that such an early exile from parents eliminates three-quarters of the year living with your family. The British, who have a corner on the boarding school trade, are rethinking the tradition that some have called institutionalized child abandonment. I wouldn't go that far, but for adventure-loving teenagers like Greg Keller and Pat Hickey, it was balls to the walls in the middle of Berkeley in the '60's without a hell of lot of parental supervision.

In the one period of life when you least want parents around, it may be the time that teenagers need them the most. Or so we thought when our oldest daughter, Shinae, was invited to join the Kirov Ballet Academy in Washington, D.C., at the age of 13. We decided not to send her and she became a cheerleader instead of a ballerina. The result: we enjoyed her high school years at home with us, even when she didn't.

A boy's boarding school makes you long for a lot of things you don't have. Having a car was number one, with female contact of any kind a close second. Even though the Christian Brothers had committed to a vow of foregoing such mysteries of the latter; they understood that an occasional chaperoned meeting of boys and girls would likely keep down the incidences of late-night shaving-cream fights and waste-can fires in the dorm.

Once a year, the proper young ladies of nearby St. Joseph's School for Girls would grace St. Mary's smelly gym with their perfumed presence. We'd all act as if it was no big deal, but secretly each freshman boarder was after-shaving his brains out in nervous anticipation of a would-be dance encounter with someone other than his 24/7 male companions.

That night I bumped into a girl who had gone to St. Theresa's at the Lake. She was a sophomore, and miles ahead of me in social skills. It was nice to finish the evening's last slow dance with someone of the opposite sex. Seeing her again was beyond me. She had other feelings and turned them into a chain of near psychotic love letters that never seemed to stop. My roommates found them amusing, which was their way of disguising the jealousy they felt since no girl had ever sent them such crazy letters. I trust Karen one day found someone capable of reciprocating her romantic zeal.

When the drought between dances went too long, the Administration found another way to deal with excess male testosterone. They would periodically schedule a Catholic school version of *Friday Night Fights*. Not the black-and-white television boxing you were accustomed to watching with your dad; these matches pitted friend against foe, friend against friend, or you against whomever Brother Richard thought could teach you the best lesson on humility that week. From the experience I learned: a boxing ring is small, boxing gloves are heavy and a three-minute round is one hell of a long time—especially if you're getting the bejesus beaten out of you.

Pat Lewis was a new friend from Napa, the home of Northern California's largest mental hospital. Not to imply his lineage descended from thereabouts, but Lewis acted like a crazy man the night he and I got into the ring. About twenty-five pounds heavier, he completely ignored the Marquess of Queensbury's rules for boxing etiquette. Dispensing with the customary opening jab, Pat floored me in the first five seconds with an overhand right. Avoiding a week of embarrassment, I beat the count and am told made a pretty good fight of that three-round eternity Lewis and I spent together.

The occasional fights, our weekend jaunts, and the late night discourses on life made for a brotherly bond that only the military or a boarding school can give a young man. Absent family, friends became the center of a dorm life that was a microcosm of the Catholic version of the Kingdom. That kingdom would later be undermined by pedophile scandals that would shake its 2,000-year-old foundations. But in those early days of the '60's, the good Christian Brothers who tended us seemed morally above reproach. Well, there was one old Brother we were afraid to approach. He sat long hours in the basement typing room waiting for boys to visit for the extra keyboard work they needed. I know from my subsequent years as a Unificationist that being singularly dedicated to a belief can, at the very least, be lonely. Probably that's all it was, but Brother A's long fingernails and propensity to touch kept us from ever becoming good typists.

Given Christ's great commission to love one's enemy, school officials were reluctant to give someone the boot. Instead, the time-honored Catholic tradition calls for the unworthy to simply not be "invited to return." This was the case for most of my fellow Tahoe classmates. Their "mountain man" mentality, combined with the urge to own a Chevy and chase girls, sealed their return to public school. I didn't fall into the unwanted category, but as I said earlier in matters religious, I tended to side with my friends. There would be no more Bells of St. Mary's for me either after my sophomore year of high school.

Leaving Catholic boarding school, I took with me fond memories, more questions than answers about faith, and above-average academic habits from the endless hours of mandatory study hall. Long hours in the smoking lounge choked me permanently on tobacco. St. Mary's gave me a leg up in the classroom my junior year back at Tahoe. It also made me the new boy in school in an old school environment. I'd attempt to use that advantage with teachers and girls. One of the unintended consequences of attending a boarding school was the newfound independence I felt from my parents. Accompanying me home with my baggage from St. Mary's was a greater distance from my family, even though I once again lived in the same house with them.

11

▼

South Tahoe Viking

RETURNING BACK TO MY FUTURE at the Lake, Mother Nature invited innocence for a return engagement. Home again and driving on a moonlit night through Hope Valley was all sparkle and light. You could turn off the car lights and drive by the reflection of the moon off the snow. In those school-day nights before Grover Hot Springs became a State Park it was little more than a literal local's hot spot in a far-off corner of the Toiyabe Forest. Devoid of the paved road that brings you there today, we'd trudge the last mile in knee-deep snow to reach Markleville's steaming jewel of the night. The shocking difference between winter's fresh powder and the 104 temperature of the springs literally took your breath away; which is what being sixteen should be all about.

Then there was the night in Hope Valley that wasn't so bright. One summer afternoon a few members of the South Tahoe baseball team and I took my '64 black Volkswagen and went fishing at a favorite lake. Overloading the back seat of the Bug, someone bruised the battery on the ride up and we were left electricity-free, eight miles above the Blue Lakes cutoff. On that overcast eve, there was no moon or shinning snow to illuminate the walk out. Stumbling on rocks that reached out to grab your feet like granite gnomes, the four of us linked up like the Rockettes to keep from marching off the edge of the road. Singing Creedence Clearwater tunes and intermittent cussing shortened the journey. Battery failure brought male bonding till the stumble fest finally finished six hours later. Reaching the junction exhausted at 4:00 a.m., we found the highway curb made an excellent pillow. A blackjack dealer on his way to work at one of the clubs honked and hauled us home. After the expected rant from my father, we brought Larry Martin's truck and a jumper cable back the next day to Blue Lakes to revive my glad-to-see us VW. Unfortunately, not all our teenage trips together were quite as idyllic.

Spring baseball at South Tahoe High was more like a combination of ice hockey and mud wrestling than the national pastime. A layer of permafrost covered the outfield. The infield resembled the frozen tundra at Lambeau Field. For early season practices, the team would head to the desert east of Carson City. The rival Dayton Dust Devils would lend us their drier diamond for weekend play. One day, guys brought their .22 rifles along for the ride. After the day's scrimmage, we piled in the back of George Downey's pick-up to ostensibly go Jack Rabbit hunting. No one before or after the great Daniel Boone has ever managed to shoot a Jack Rabbit with anything other than a shotgun; so it shouldn't surprise anyone that our bunny safari didn't produce the intended results. Unfortunately, or fortunately, depending on how you view such matters, there were other nearby adventures in the desert waiting to befall us. One of the senior outfielders suggested a truth-or-dare session over at the Moonlite Ranch.

For those who don't know about Nevada's brothel industry,

whorehouses have been operating in the Silver State since the middle of the 19th Century. Realizing the Federal Government was looking to shut down gambling itself during its Mob-infested early days, state officials allowed only the rural "cow counties" to legalize Nevada's second most famous vice. Moonlite was a poor stepchild of the more infamous Mustang Ranch near Reno.

Avoiding eye contact and making poor attempts at man humor, most of the team watched as a few puffed-up young stallions turned over their dollars to the Madam inside that trailer of iniquity. Names have been forgotten to protect the innocence that was lost. One boy, minus bravado, confessed he kept his socks on during the mostly sordid affair. A metaphor for purity now breached, his white socks were a remnant of the decency that even a $10 lay couldn't remove.

Our boys' basketball team was every bit as pitiful to watch. Short shorts may look good on girls, but men's butt-hugging trunks looked as bad on us as they one day would on Larry Bird. The Hip Hop generation has at least lowered the threshold of how much of a man's hairy legs you are required to view during a game. Still, my South Tahoe Vikings' greatest nemesis wasn't the tightness of our pants, but the quality of our play. Like our Nordic namesakes, we were better at winter sports than hoops. It showed up big time on the court, even when we played teams like the Braves from the Stewart Indian School.

The Stewart Indians had a unique style and a definite home-court advantage. Besides better dribbling, crisper bounce passing and deadly outside shooting, they managed to make us look like scarecrows flailing in the wind whenever they passed the ball between our legs. The Stewart fans were worthy of the NBA 6th-man award. From their Hoosier-like gym balcony, they'd encircle visiting white teams like their ancestors did our great grandparents' pioneer wagons. Camped in the paint, you'd get ambushed with whatever the female fans could find to throw. Unlike the Wild West, their referees, not ours, were judge and jury. In retaliation for the many sins of the white men, we were spit on, taunted and even tripped by the Indian cheerleaders. In the end, the Shoshone and Paiute fans seemed content with their team's massacre of the hapless Vikings. During such moments of agony and defeat, I was taught an invaluable lesson about the restoration of historic resentments. Pay the indemnity for the collective sins of your forbearers—and get the hell out of the gym!

You've already heard about the environmental challenges and extra-curricular exploits of the baseball team. Let me now tell you about the games themselves. I do so having a unique perspective–firmly attached to the end of the bench. Riding the pine my junior season, we accumulated long slivers and a short attention span. The game of baseball, being slow, provides plenty of time for contemplation, jawboning and the creation of your own secret society of benchwarmers. Nothing elaborate or self-important—we were simply the Goon Squad. Certain low standards were upheld as a proud member of the "gooners." The foremost being, you were never to be paying attention when the coach called your name. That virtue alone guaranteed a lifetime membership on the squad, especially as far as Coach Bill Miller was concerned.

Marty Hoch, one of the founding Goon Squad members, had an odd distinguishing behavior of frequently displaying his hind side to the public. The original "moonie" as far as I'm concerned, Marty would bid farewell to opposing teams with his signature moon over Manhattan pose in the back window of our departing bus. He eventually got caught and was suspended from school. Personally, I would have loved to have been a fly on the wall the day his dad got that call from Principal Downey. "He did what?" In the 1990's, Marty would have been enrolled in a twelve-step program for butt wavers. Back then, he simply had to grow up. Marty did, and went on to be a successful family and business man in Sacramento. Still though, at every class reunion he entertains requests for an encore performance.

12

My Mother

WRITING ABOUT ADOLESCENT INCIDENTS back in my school days is easy for me now. Speaking about them to my parents at the time would have been impossible. I might have talked but they couldn't listen. I could have unloaded, but the heavy lifting of a teenage burden was more than they were braced to handle. Parents weren't yet into relating to the traumas of their teens. Transparency wasn't yet in style. Hypocrisy was; but like all its victims, they weren't aware of it. Trying to bury their own bugaboos, most parents weren't ready to exchange them with their young.

Teenagers themselves during the Depression, my mother and father were understandably preoccupied with the material side of life. Striving for wealth and keeping up appearances in the eyes of their friends were important values to their generation. Unlike my '60's cohorts, our parents looked at the status quo as something to aspire to, not spurn.

I've not spoken a lot about my mother. Mom loved me in ways that seemed, at times, too much. She had a hard life before marrying my father. Her failed first marriage and the burden of raising my sister alone made her emotionally vulnerable and extremely strong-minded. Over time, my Father's kindness and acceptance of my sister as a daughter helped Mom to recover.

So did being at the center of all things that were social at the South Shore. She managed the women's clothing department at upscale Joseph Magnin's near the casinos. There she met and befriended many of Tahoe's silver mavens of style. The ladies gathered at each other's homes for weekly bridge games in a moveable feast of light sandwiches and heavy gossip. Gossip works best when the racy tidbits tossed into the rumor mill are about someone else's offspring. Over the years, my list of exploits and the subsequent buzz that I'd dropped out of college, refused the draft, bought a Volkswagen Bus, became a ski bum and joined the Moonies turned the focus from finger sandwiches–to her boy.

For that boy, the scarcity of spiritual nourishment at the dinner table left me hungering for sustenance of a more internal nature. Granted, only those with more than enough to eat can contemplate the poverty of the heart. Still, there were nights I was ready to admit my fears and confess my sins in return for my parents' forgiveness and advice. It was probably better I didn't. My folks weren't emotionally equipped to deal with my anguish. How could they have known the answers to questions they'd never asked themselves? The irony would be evident years later when I thought I'd answered all of life's important questions; and my two sons never asked.

Worrying tops the list of a job description of parenting. My mother was overqualified in that department. Her worrying didn't necessarily bother me. She had good reason to. But worrying about what others thought always bothered me and gave me an excuse to not listen to her warnings. I'm sorry for the worrying that was unwarranted–the kind that requires patience to see the end game–of a boy becoming a man. I'm in search of that patience tonic myself, as I try to improve on those easier-said-than-done parenting skills with my own four children.

My wife says a mother's birthing ordeal is forgotten the moment the newborn is placed in her arms. The child delivers a healing balm in the tears that stream down a new mother's face. Long after my mother gave birth to me, I returned pain to her for years. I doubt most of the tears she shed healed her worried heart. I hope that she somehow realized before she died that most of the pain I gave her was simply from me trying to give birth to my self.

13

The Music

MY MOTHER AND HER HIGH-SOCIETY friends weren't the only ones engaged in regular Tahoe social gatherings. For my crowd, there was the American Legion Hall. The musical venue featured the locals' favorite, the Jim Burgett Band. Content to play *Louie, Louie* and Sam and Dave tunes till the midnight hour, their tunes provided background noise for the dance floor fights that took place faithfully every Saturday night. There were three essential ingredients for a teenage scuffle at the Legion Hall: locals, tourists and an overabundance of Coors consumed by both. The volatile combination of the three produced a predictable rumble with chairs tossed and punches thrown—all timed to give Jim and his horn section a cigarette break. The El Dorado Sheriff's Office had a standing order to come around 11:00 p.m. and haul a few bloodied bodies off. Following the sheriffs' appearance, dancing resumed.

By my senior year, a new musical wind had blown into town from San Francisco. Having just changed their name from the Warlocks, the Grateful Dead appeared one Saturday night at Tahoe's American Legion Hall–inadvertently bringing peace to the place. Actually, the guys from the football team wanted to punch them out but the band's weirdness kept the jocks off balance. Contributing to the brawl-free night were the long guitar solos of Jerry Garcia. We were accustomed to hearing forty-five seconds of crisp Fender riffs followed by a hasty return to a song's lyrics. The guys in the Dead kept jamming, oblivious to the audience's bewilderment, as if they were in some drug-induced trance; which of course they were. Gawking at the Dead's tie-died patulli oil-smelling tee-shirts, there was little time to pick a fight with a tourist from the Bay Area.

We did manage to get under organist Pig Pen's tattooed skin when he left the Hall to take up with a bunch of black groupies waiting in a flophouse behind the dance hall. Linda Lindsay lined up along the rear exit and thought she'd embarrass Old Pig by sarcastically commenting on his white afro by remarking, "Nice hair!" That resulted in an f-you response that we all agreed was quite remarkable for a guy to say to a girl in those days–even a long-haired pot-smoking scum like Pig Pen. In spite of our indifference, the Dead would return, along with the Jefferson Airplane, the Quicksilver Messenger Service, Santana, Janis Joplin and a host of other psychedelic gypsies, each attempting to get us to just say no to fighting and yes to taking drugs.

At 17, I wasn't quite ready to come under their influence. Another Saturday night at the Legion Hall, one of my fellow ski-team members tried to put a move on the girl I was dating. Our squabble didn't warrant a full-scale Legion rumble, so we took our business into the boys' bathroom. I let go with a stunning right cross for Gary's chin. Unfortunately it got caught up in the hanging cloth towel dispenser and barely connected. Before I knew it we were in the holding tank in the El Dorado County Jail. My foe's father arrived and acted like a teenager's dream dad; he shrugged it off and was seen laughing as he drove my co-combatant home. I wasn't in for the same nonchalant response from my parents. That particular Saturday evening in late January happened to be my Mother's birthday, making the timing of my chivalrous defense of my date's honor ill-chosen, to say the least. I presented my mother the gift of a jail visitation on an otherwise joyous occasion. Along with the obligatory two-week grounding that followed, I was left with the image of that hanging towel and what a tremendous job it did of blocking my punch.

I've already chronicled how many of my father's business decisions were ill-advised. Having barely passed Mr. Cortez's Introduction to Business class the previous spring, a friend and I were about to demonstrate how I'd inherited his genes. Chris Mozley and I decided on a summer business venture that would put what little economic theory we knew into practice. The first mistake we made was in the naming of the company. An odd-jobs attempt, we christened the endeavor *Favors Unlimited* on business cards we circulated around homes on the South Shore.

Our first job came from a kindly old New Age devotee who needed dirt removed from under the foundation of his house in order to get an FHA loan. He enticed us into an agreement by promising his wife would feed us lunch each day along with the $250 that would be deposited in our pockets when the job was done. His wife's organic sandwiches turned out to be delicious; but our cost calculations made us sick. Chris and I spent the better part of our summer vacation under the old geezer's house looking like coal miners hauling dirt out in shoeboxes. When all was said and done, our take came out to be something like six cents an hour; proving, at least, that we'd selected the right name for our company.

14

Favors Unlimited

WHEN ALL ELSE FAILED, as Favors Unlimited most certainly did, there was always my Father's ice truck to drive. No longer stuck inside the cold-storage warehouse bagging cubes, I was now old enough to drive around the Lake during the summer months melting them. My grandfather's previous customers with the Scotch stash had long since passed away, but there were still contemporary perks to be had in delivering ice in the 1960's. Casino walk-in freezers were an all-you-can-eat freeloader's buffet. I could feast on beef before it was introduced to Stroganoff, grab a handful of strawberries before they topped the shortcake and generally indulge in whatever was edible or could fit in my pocket. Delivering ice for my father's business, I learned a lot; how to deal with people, keep track of money and make a trip back from Fallen Leaf Lake take twice as long as it was supposed to. I also learned I didn't want to be a third-generation proprietor of the Hickey Ice Company. Higher education would offer alternatives, even if high school at STHS seemed geared to distract you from that goal.

The '60's being about experimentation, the administration at South Tahoe High School got the liberal notion that restructuring class schedules along the lines of a university curriculum would prepare us to better deal with time management responsibilities in college and later in life. Combined with an open-campus policy for those with mag wheels, "modular scheduling" turned out to be an invitation for fugitives on the lam from class to intern down at the local pool hall with shark emeritus, Larry Leonardo. Having my afternoons freed up by Principal Downey's generous notion of irresponsibility for the senior class, I acquired a minor in nine-ball to go along with my South Tahoe diploma. Thank God I always had a job to fall back on because Larry and a certain pinball machine took all of my spare change every time I went in there.

Visiting 40 years later, the campus that was once new – the trees and buildings – are still there, both having grown old. Even the great pine that stood next to the Principal's office has been topped, like most '60's standards that have been removed. The seeds of my generation's follies can be seen in the era of political correctness that succeeded us. In the window of Mr. Cortez's old business classroom is taped the words "Safe Zone." Meaning, I presume, that inside those four walls now a 17 year-old is guaranteed to study in an environment that, "Respects all aspects of people, including race, ethnicity, gender expression, sexual orientation, socio-economic background, age religion, body shape, size and ability." If those standards had been in place in 1968 for the crowd I hung with, we wouldn't have known what to do. There wouldn't have been anyone, including ourselves, to make fun of.

15

Work

WORK IS IN MY BLOOD. With all of it I've done, it's surprising I'm not permanently on workers' comp. My employment history began with selling chocolate mints for St. Theresa's and eating most of the profits. I bagged, cut and delivered ice for my father's business every summer from the time I was nine. I dug ditches, cut lawns and slept on the job for the Lake Tahoe School District. I worked at Nel's Hardware Store for Kenny Caple's dad, never figuring out what aisle nails were on before I was let go. Hauling dirty sheets for Larry Martin's dry-cleaning business was mustier than you might imagine. I worked for Randy Koller's dad one summer as a plumber's helper. My position was at the wrong end of a stupid stick learning what every plumber knows—that shit flows downhill and paydays, regardless of how small, are on Friday. A summer of love for some, it was a summer of blisters for me. Caesar Chavez protested, but I sold lettuce for Bonanza Produce. I delivered drugs in college. Not for a dealer, but for a pharmacy. Dish washing was my specialty in Bradley Hall at Chico State, a grueling perk in lieu of them not having money for skiing scholarships. I got certified and taught skiing at Homewood Resort at the Lake while studying at Chico. I dug ditches and blew up dynamite before a ski season in the early '70's in the Wasatch Mountain Range in Utah. One of my ditch-mates looked and sounded exactly like Richard Nixon; which was not to his advantage during the Watergate era. After getting robbed in a Waikiki church, I worked for Portuguese Gomes in a Honolulu fish market long enough to earn money to get a plane ticket home. I skinned elk and moose in a hunting camp near Jackson, Wyoming; or at least until the maggots got under my skin. I was a night bellman at Snowbird Lodge in Alta Utah, the first season it opened. During the day I marauded as a helicopter powder guide for the rich and famous, such as Bobby Kennedy's son. I worked again as a ski instructor back at Heavenly Valley, trying to mend things with my parents before I left home for good. I worked for God in the Unification Church. He didn't pay much but promised a great benefits package in the next life. In the Movement, I did corporate fundraising for UNICEF on Wall Street, sold flowers on the streets of New York's Chinatown, and resurrected my career as a chocolate salesman, once again eating a good portion of God's inventory. One night while fundraising in Tony Soprano's neighborhood in New Jersey, I stumbled into a Mafia card game. An aspiring Made-man laid down his straight flush and pointed a gun at my head. Since I'd punched in on God's time clock, I figured getting wacked would qualify as a martyr's death. He didn't shoot and I'm still working off bad karma. While at a seminary in upstate New York, I moonlighted on weekends selling gold chains by the inch to Guido's at a Long Island flea market. I trust if this ever gets published, I'll have some lifetime warranty issues with a few working-class Italian-Americans with green chains in Hempstead. I served as a Director for Project Volunteer in the Cabrini Green Housing Projects in Chicago distributing mountains of excess government cheese. Marie Antoinette may or may not have uttered "let them eat cake." But whichever Washington bureaucrat came up with the idea of processed American cheese combating poverty, he was just as clueless. I crewed on a church member's shrimp boat in Galveston, Texas. Forrest Gump Shrimp we were not, but I've never tasted crustacean any better than freshly cooked on a shrimp boat's grumbling old manifold. I worked out getting delivery trucks donated to Cecil Murray's First A.M.E. Church in Los Angeles so the Hollywood elite could feel good about themselves in the wake of the Rodney King riots. I became a Northern California campaign manager for Bruce Herschensohn's failed U.S. Senate try in California. I later did the same when Cheryl Lau tried for governor in Nevada. I served as a liaison to the public-relations firm of Huckaby and Rodriguez in Sacramento as they tried to do for the Moonies what they had done for the Mormons: make them acceptable. That job remains unfinished. I was appointed a Western States Director for the Movement's lobbying organization, the American Constitution Committee. It was a non-profit organization in more ways than one. I started a painting business in Carson City without knowing the difference between latex and semi-gloss. The company now grosses over two million annually—proving that even ignorance sometimes gets rewarded. I worked as an intern for Nevada Assemblyman Lou Bergevin. Possessing enormous political balls, I once heard him tell Vegas casino mogul Steve Wynn to take a flying leap while discussing Wynn's casino fine-art tax scam. The internship pay was nonexistent, but the lessons were priceless. Rush Limbaugh, whom I'd known in Sacramento, helped me land a job at KOH Radio in Reno as a political reporter. I eventually syndicated my report to eight stations from Las Vegas to the cow counties. Reporting about the Legislature, I got offered a columnist position with Carson City's *Nevada Appeal*. The pay was about as good as working for God, but it propelled me into getting elected to the part-time Nevada Legislature. That paid about as much as being a missionary; but boy was it memorable. After my flash-in-the-pan political career ended, I took a position as editor of the *Nevada Journal,* a public policy magazine riding herd on a bunch of cranky libertarian writers. Last summer I apprenticed with a general contractor who built our mountain cabin on the Little Walker River. We both agreed that if he ever was to pay me, I'd be about a $6.00-an-hour guy.

The hardest job on my resume has been raising four kids. I can only hope they'd hire me again.

16

Teenage Romance

BLESSED TO BE IN A RELATIONSHIP with a woman in marriage for thirty years has removed most memories of before. Being in a lifetime of love has completed what was partial about my past. Still, I can't leave high school without telling you about a girl. She was pretty and petite, the kind of girl most guys would crave the attention of in the hallway between classes. Having just come from St. Mary's, I was new in school and to her. There was chemistry in class and she made the first moves. We went together to proms, parties and stolen days at Hidden Beach reveling in newfound teenage affections. As Bob Seger sang, the two of us became an item in the "front page drive-in news." My mother didn't care for her. Much in the same way she didn't care for any female that competed for her affections. Myung-Hee would one day overcome that. But that's a later story.

First love opens a spigot. But at age sixteen, the emotional well was too shallow to sustain it. The gusher of previously untapped feelings inevitably clogged. The adolescent hormones and dreams that drew us

together later pulled us apart. We were both good students
to become teachers. I cried the night we left separately for
wrote in my yearbook that she would always love me. Seei _
high-school reunions, it seemed as if it might have been true.

My high school flame had this recurring dream of a dark figure
coming to drag her away in the night. I had nightmares of my own
when she left with his representative in our second year of college.
I was looking at a prison term for refusing induction into the Army
when I got the break-up call. Walls came crashing down, as only they
can at nineteen. Dealing with the devastation, I tried drowning my
misery listening to everything from Lenny Bruce to Led Zeppelin.
Laughter easily turned to tears as I got stuck between comedy and a
hard rock-place in my attempts at self-therapy.

Spend enough time with a broken heart and you'll get introspective.
The '60's went from thoughts of the world–to the 70's, and thinking
about self. Free love was costly. Many turned inward when we couldn't
pay the bill. As if to prove the point, my high-school sweetheart would
become a devotee of the Maharishi; and I found Reverend Moon.
Strangely, I'm now grateful for her infidelity. I'd never be as happy
as I am today without being leveled by my limitations then. Youthful
indiscretions spared me to love fully in the future.

A few years ago I received a late-night call from her last male
companion telling me of her death. I said a quiet prayer, knowing the
dark visitor had finally taken her away.

17

▼

Faithlessness

TRADITIONAL FAITH HAD ITS LAST FLING with me in high school. Soon everything and everyone that was a part of the Establishment would be suspect. Good Friday, if you can call the day the man from Nazareth was murdered a good one, is a solemn Catholic Holy Day you spend quietly with your thoughts as you make the Stations of the Cross. Not much pomp and ceremonial circumstance involved, you prayerfully make the rounds of Christ's Passion–reflecting on his suffering. Minus the gore of Mel Gibson's version, the Church's historic wood carvings in St. Theresa's helped worshippers dwell on the sorrowful path that led to Christ's crucifixion.

The Easter Friday of my senior year, I came upon my own Road to Damascus experience. Rather than confronting the persecutor in Saul, Christ challenged the doubting Thomas in me.

When God decides to deliver a message, there's a universe of resources at His disposal. Back in the time of Moses—a burning bush was the preferred medium. During Jesus' time, hovering white doves were a favorite courier. And besides mediocre attempts at movie-making with the likes of George Burns and Morgan Freeman in the lead role, His best contemporary conduit would probably be a music channel. Given that most young people listen to about four hours of mindless melodies a day, God can always drop in a few lyrics to get His message across. He did so for me anyway. While making my altar-boy rounds at Good Friday's Stations of the Cross, I thought of Dion's classic tune, "Abraham, Martin and John." It's the song about Abraham Lincoln, Martin Luther King and John F. Kennedy and "how it seems the good they die young." It occurred to me that Jesus should have been added to the song like Bobby Kennedy later was.

After the Good Friday service, I sat there in a pew pondering about who Jesus was and why He died. I thought if he truly was God, then all the temptations and struggles of the flesh were just a formality of sorts, since He was bound to overcome them by the mere fact of Divine design. If He couldn't, then the idea of Heaven and salvation were a moot point spelling hopelessness for the mortal man. In spite of a Catechism upbringing with three-in-one oil equaling the Trinity analogies, it was confusing trying to comprehend a "glorious mystery" who was both man and God. If everything that happened to Him—his rejection, betrayal, and death was merely the plot of the greatest story ever told—then why feel remorse on Good Friday? It was all predestined to happen anyway. From that day on, I decided I related to Jesus better as him than Him.

Sitting alone after the Service, I had other-worldly thoughts about my life. I wondered who would attend my funeral when I died. What would they remember and say about me? I was overcome with emotion, feeling that if I died at that moment, no one I was close to would know how much I cared for them. I saw myself speaking at my own Irish Wake and making the last thing I ever said to anyone being an affirmation of love. That subliminal take was probably from some Lennon/McCartney song and not the Man upstairs. Still, having a brush with conscience at sixteen is a good thing, even if it leaves you with troubling afterthoughts. My teenage epiphany gave way to more secular sentiments. Following my session with life's sixty-four-thousand-dollar questions, I left St. Theresa's for a party at Rick Bates' house with Greg Keller and my theological advisors.

18

Party School U.S.A.

HIGH SCHOOL FINISHED WITH A BLAZE of parties and bon voyages in the form of makeshift "Last Will and Testaments" in the back of the yearbook. Arrogantly informing anyone bothering to read such nonsense, I bequeathed "a cool breeze to anyone who passed up on my friendship." Good thing I was graduating. Otherwise, I'd have probably gotten rolled in the hall the following year by the junior class.

Leaving the comfort zone of friends is like being born. You kick and scream your way out the dark door of the familiar before growing up in the bright unknown. A new college environment may hold more promise for the future, but kids' first reaction is to stick close to the womb-like security of the old high school crowd. That was true for a lot of my friends and the reason so many came home to Tahoe on weekends. I figured my lifelong friends would be just that. I looked forward for reasons not to return.

Believe it or not, I wasn't aware at the time I applied to Chico State that it had been voted *Playboy Magazine*'s undisputed top party school that year. That fact was later underscored by my experiences at the now-banned Pioneer Days celebrations. Not knowing of the brews and bikinis awaiting an awkward freshman, I choose Chico because of the fond memories I had there as a child with my elderly grandparents.

Nineteen sixty-eight was a chaotic year to begin college. Three hours from Berkeley, fashionable radicalism was migrating north by counterculture osmosis. Like every college freshman, I was petrified my first day in class. Scared even more by English Professor Tom Reck's assignment of an in-class essay, I figured I was about to demonstrate how much my scholarly skills had slipped since attending St. Mary's. Proving that his long hair and Fu Manchu mustache symbolized his anti-establishment sentiments, the good professor wrote on the blackboard the first day's topic: "Who do you think would make a better President, Richard Nixon or Mickey Mouse?" By the way, some thirty-four years later Dr. Reck's photo appears with a Mickey statue on his website–indicating he was, in fact, a true believer in the Great Leader of the Mousketeers. Dumbstruck, students didn't know whether to laugh or ask him if he was kidding. Reck didn't give anyone the chance to assess his motives or clarify his expectations. He left the room, and for the next 55 minutes we were left with either taking him seriously or failing our first university assignment. Not remembering what nonsense I wrote, I'm sure it didn't matter to him as long as it was grammatically sound and didn't offend his political sensibilities.

Then there was the Political Science Department's openly Marxist professor who parroted the '60's anthem of "power to the people" whenever he spoke. He was a faculty advisor for one of Chico State's earliest environmental organizations, "Save our Seashore" (S.O.S.). Chico is about 150 miles inland from the Pacific Coast, so I never understood why the California coastline was his pet cause. Regardless, it worked. We wrote angry letters to big oil companies that spilled their product on sea birds and baby seals along the Santa Barbara Coast. No one knows if the letters helped, but directing our anger toward someone we considered evil made us feel good about ourselves.

I enjoyed the mad Marxist's rants on the plight of the proletariat, which as a poor college student I suppose I was a part of. He was especially convincing when railing against the alleged egomaniacs running the Military Industrial Complex. Having attended an organizational meeting of S.O.S., I realized it took one to know one. In my increasingly disillusioned view, the only thing larger than his inflated ego was the Pentagon's defense budget. Critical thinking was an esteemed virtue of our progressive professors. As long as you were critical of the right folks, you were guaranteed of getting good grades, even though most leftist academics detested the capitalist grading system that rewarded anyone who achieved.

I don't want you to think that just because I attended a California University in the late '60's, I gave up all my traditional values. Beer drinking, frat parties and fantasizing about pretty co-eds were still core beliefs of the Chico Wildcats I befriended my freshman year at Bradley Hall. Bradley was one of the newer dorms on campus, strategically located near the TKE House and next to one of Chico's endless almond orchards. The TKE's were challenging the Lambda Pi's as the Greek System's rowdiest party animals on campus. This resulted in beer keggers being thrown every weekend at their frat house. The endless rows of trees provided late-night revelers with a strategic escape route back to the dorms once Chico's Finest arrived on the scene.

Having already spent two of my high school years crammed in a dorm room, I was anxious to make friends with other guys who had similar notions of a great escape. The summer before our sophomore year, Rob Orr from Napa and I went door-to-door like Mormon missionaries trying to find a house to convert. We found the perfect pre-gentrified shack on the wrong side of Chico's railroad tracks and on right side of the Wonder Bread Bakery, where we got our daily day-old bread. After moving in that fall, the four of us deliberated over a few beers before christening our new abode, "Sweet Dump." A sign was painted sloppily and hung crookedly over the dilapidated front porch. Thirty-nine years later the home is still there on Second Street, having been properly gentrified by a college administrator and his wife.

"Sweet Dump" (I am standing on the left)
Chico, 1969

In keeping with its Dump motif, we landscaped the front yard with empty Coors cans and a failed attempt at a corn crop. The priest at the nearby Newman Center was constantly upset with us, not so much for our moral transgressions but because we soiled his sensibilities as a member of the Sierra Club. The backyard, however, was solely dedicated to Nature; meaning we never cut the grass. A good thing, because my roommate John from Orinda was a falconer and kept his Red-tailed Hawk tethered back there. The tall grass provided the bird of prey cover from which to attack the girl next door's cat. We were slightly more humane with regard to dogs. The sorority girls on the other side of the Dump had a sweet little black puppy they pampered until it stopped being cute. We took in the orphaned mutt and aptly named him Rat Pup. Like his masters and our digs, he wasn't quite ready for *Sunset Magazine.*

The other member of the Dump's menagerie was a turtle named Tommy. A large desert variety, he helped keep down our electrical costs. We'd attach a candle to his shell and give him lettuce to devour, which would typically provide about a half hour of light and a stoner's notion of entertainment. Another way we saved money was never to buy dishwashing soap. About the only time dishes would get washed was when someone's parents came to town and we had to put up a pretense of being human. Girls rarely visited–something about the décor. Another pathetic facet of our domestic regimen was how we managed the refrigerator. Influenced by our professors, the four of us were fairly egalitarian in the early months of our time there together. For example: Steve, our resident Jewish guitarist would frequently splurge on milk and eggs and actually be quite generous with their distribution. Later, after all of us had read Any Rand's *Atlas Shrugged,* it was every individual for himself. By then we'd reached the zenith of personal anarchy and ridiculousness. Margaret Mead surely observed such adolescent behavior in most primitive college settings.

Having been the on the house search committee, I was entitled to the first pick of a bedroom at the Dump. I choose the screened-in summer porch in the rear of the house. There I built a loft for my bed over the makeshift desk of an old door on cinder blocks. What my engineering feat didn't take into account was the wide range of Chico's temperatures. Enclosing the loft, I took away the advantage of the screens, causing me to boil half the year and freeze the other. There was a silver lining in my inability to get enough sleep. Self-inflicted sleep deprivation turned out to be a useful skill later in life as a Unification fundraiser.

One of the more fashionable courses to take in 1969 was Eastern Religions. Western religions were passé to most of us in the '60's crowd. Sgt. Pepper was more popular than Jesus, at least for a while. Many of us were curious to see if the spiritual grass was greener on the other side of the world-religions globe.

I expected the professor to be robed, beaded and titled Shri-Baba something. To everyone's surprise, he entered the classroom sporting a conservative suit, horn-rimmed glasses and a crew cut. Preconceptions aside, he proceeded to lead the class on a fascinating journey through the various Eastern faiths. He taught each tradition with such clarity and passion that when he'd finished a section, students would be convinced he really was a Buddhist or a Hindu. He promised to answer at the end of the semester the question every one of us had, "Which one do you believe in?"

Paradoxes being part of the Eastern mystique, he dropped a bombshell on the last day of class when he confessed that he was nothing more than a drab Presbyterian fascinated by the faith of others. The irony was lost on most. But it occurred to me that his respect for other beliefs spoke volumes about the faith he kept to himself. Or maybe our WASP instructor was just practicing what Taoist Lao Tzu taught, "He who says does not know and he who knows does not say." Country and Western guru Allison Krause revealed the same esoteric knowledge when she sang, "You say it best when you say nothing at all." His evenhanded approach to the touchy subject of religion made him the wonderful teacher he was. The kind every nineteen year-old deserves to get at least once during their time in college.

Teachers were like gods to me. I viewed their podiums as pedestals, placing most of them on high. Never imagining one day a teacher might knock the bloom off my rosy view, I went to college dreaming of becoming one.

In my sophomore year at Chico, a relationship developed with a professor that affected forever what I thought about those I placed my hopes in. Space in his creative writing classes was a privilege coveted by many and enjoyed by few. Writing for him went light years beyond working for a grade. Assignments became a literary vision quest seeking his seal of approval. We wrote to gain entry into the inner sanctum of his thoughts. Every member of our seminar group felt connected to the soul of the man. Even his red-pen critiques were an invitation to discourse with a figure who, I dare say, had become so close he felt like a friend.

When the invitation came for dinner, I bought a new denim shirt for the occasion. His Tudor-style home was located north of campus near the entrance to idyllic Bidwell Park. The quiet oak-canopied street is where most of Chico's tenured academics lived. Only blocks from Sweet Dump, it was miles from where I was. Welcomed into his study before dinner, the room smelled of pipe smoke, teakwood and first editions. A glass of wine was offered. Such a gesture today would invite legal liabilities too risky for even the most liberal of professors. Then, it was a cool inducement to camaraderie offered only to a select few. Parlor pleasantries concluded, we moved to the dinning room where a lesson in life, and not Haiku, was waiting to be served.

I'd looked forward to meeting his wife. In a strange way, we'd all envied the woman none of us knew anything about. Students stood in line for an hour for ten minutes of time with her spouse. She was enjoying, or so I thought, a lifetime with the man we virtually worshipped. It would have better fit my ideal if she had been the perfect complement to his persona. I expected them to be happy. I could sense, over dinner, they were not. She seemed bored with his interests and burdened by my being there. I left the evening pleased to have entered his world and puzzled why it wasn't what I imagined. In a funny way, I blamed her for not appreciating him the way we did. A few months later at a university ski meet, I met the pretty young coed likely responsible for her aloofness.

19

Refusing America

THE ZODIAC WAS BIG NEWS THAT YEAR in Northern California. But something more catastrophic than the crazed serial killer or my professor's marital problems was taking place in Southeast Asia that would affect me for years. The North Vietnamese Tet Offensive in 1968 led LBJ and his generals to believe the U.S. needed more than the 500,000 troops deployed in order to win the war. Social critics were quick to point out that America's poor and rural young were dying in far greater numbers than her more "fortunate sons" like myself. Campuses traditionally being a safe haven for the country's economic elite were the best place to rectify that social inequity. To that end, something happened while in college I never expected. I got drafted.

That winter night the news came, I thought of my father. He'd done his duty when World War II came knocking. It had never occurred to me I'd do anything less. Then again, it was the '60's, and I was listening to Country Joe McDonald's "I Feel Like I'm Fixin'-to-Die Rag" and not "When Johnny Comes Marching Home." Many brave American sons followed in their World War II fathers' footsteps to Vietnam. I wasn't one of them.

In California, especially, my generation was in revolt. The counterculture climate, our professors, the music and my friends all influenced my view of the world and the war. Knowing little of the evils of communism, I'd learned plenty in college about the evils of capitalism. I didn't understand the U.S.'s reasons for being in Vietnam. I barely understood my reasons for not trusting those in positions of authority. Whatever it was I believed, it went along with prevailing anti-war attitudes of most in my generation from the Golden State.

Strange in a way, because as a child I grew up playing backyard American soldier with a passion that would have made Audie Murphy proud. I had my mother sew yellow stripes on my blue jeans before reenacting a Cavalryman's response to the Battle of Little Big Horn. I wore out my Dad's old Army fatigues fighting imaginary Nazis in the make-believe Black Forest below Heavenly Valley. During the day, my battalions of plastic army men were permanently encamped in the dirt mounds outside my house re-fighting the Battle of the Bulge. My mother would have to bathe both the troops and me before bringing us inside at night before re-taking Iwo Jima from the Japanese. Greg Keller and I wore ski goggles to protect our eyes from errant bee-bee gunshots we'd fire at each other during our battles against the Chinese Communist hordes on the Bijou Golf Course. A part of the first generation to grow up watching television, I watched ABC's longest running military show, *Combat*, as devotedly as any fan of *Lost* does today.

My real-life brush with the military began on December 1, 1969. All eyes at Sweet Dump, including the turtle's, were glued to the boob tube that fateful night. So were 850,000 other draft-eligible males in America between the ages of 19 and 25. Evening classes were canceled on campuses across the country. Students and their girlfriends viewed with anxious dread the bingo-like lottery with life-and-death implications. The televised event began with a prayer and ended with a benediction. In between, college students across America pleaded for intercession from the Almighty with a passion probably not seen since the last great war. As fate would have it, my number was 154. It was in the middle, but low enough to be called the following spring. In my case, prayer was unnecessary. God surely must have been occupied answering more earnest appeals than the terrified foxhole type I would have uttered. Besides, intuition has its own channel to the future. I'd already dreamed of the day. It was just a matter of when.

Months would pass before getting drafted, taking the physical, refusing induction and going to prison. In the meantime, I faced my fears of the future increasingly alone. Doing what parents and society expect is easier on the psyche. Struggles intensified as I left the safe cocoon of the normal. Rebelling against society's norms may intrigue Hollywood. But it was anything but a blockbuster back home in Tahoe.

Troubled by the expectations attached to my parents' purse strings, I decided it was wrong to keep taking their money for school. There was no real point staying in college trying to delay the inevitable. If I was going to take a stand on what I believed about the Vietnam War, the Draft was giving me that chance. Facing the likelihood of being inducted in the spring, I decided to drop out of school. Before telling my parents, there were emotional bridges to cross and effigies of my past to burn. Going against the grain overwhelmed me at times. Then again, young men my age were being quite literally overwhelmed by the Viet Cong in the jungles of Nam.

20

The Dark Day of Altamont

As if December 1st had not been gloomy enough, four days later I joined thousands of tie-dyed soldiers of the soul to hear the Rolling Stones perform a free concert in San Francisco. I'd hoped a pilgrimage from Chico to the '60's music Mecca would help relieve me of my draft card blues. As it turned out, too many hippies descended on Golden Gate Park causing the festival to be moved to the barren blacktop basin at Altamont Speedway.

Hyped as the second coming of "Woodstock," the scene with the Stones at Altamont turned out to be a literal "Symphony for the Devil." At least, the Hells Angels lived up to their billing on that darkest of days for the love generation. Providing security for the concert, drunken members of the motorcycle gang beat the life out of eighteen-year-old African-American Meridith Hunter while Mick Jagger preened and pranced on stage.

Rock fan innocents weren't the only victims at that drug-crazed festival on December 6, 1969. The '60's died that day as well. The decade born of dreams expired like the Kennedys and King in the blood-stained arms of those who believed. If Woodstock was my generation's psychedelic flower, then Altamont was the overdose that snuffed it.

Fortunately, I ended up missing the apocalypse that was Altamont. Arriving early Saturday morning to my old stomping grounds, Berkeley was deserted and eerily quiet. Street people and students alike had migrated east to the concert. Besides, I had other things on my mind than music. Waving farewell to my roommates, I strolled along a placid Telegraph Avenue undisturbed, except for the dull ache that was now the constant companion of my stomach.

21

A Rebel with a cause but not a Movement

WANDERING AROUND BERKELEY, I entered the office of the American Friends Service Committee. Their historical opposition to violence and war was legendary and genuine. With all that I was contemplating, I needed somebody's help. A gentle Quaker staffing the desk suggested applying for Conscientious Objector status. If granted, it was an alternative to fighting by serving in a non-combatant capacity. Another alternative was to visit the less peaceful crowd down the street at the S.D.S. (Students for a Democratic Society) office.

Meeting their lone survivor from the exodus to Altamont, I found a fellow who was much more than "anti-war." He was vehemently anti-American. He advised me to take direct political action, such as burning my draft card, stealing my physical exam paperwork, disappearing in some hippie underground or fleeing to Canada. I'd planned to resist the Draft, but I wasn't prepared to turn my back on the country. I left the office feeling like I was just recruited to join SDS's political battle against the United States. A rebel with a cause but not a Movement, I decided against fighting in either side's war.

After that weekend, things were different back in Chico. My roommates had fared better in the Lottery. They had their college days and graduation to look forward to. My future was punctuated by a haunting question mark.

Home for the holidays for two weeks, life was devoid of Christmas cheer. My parents were aware of the impending Draft and how it might include me. Still, I couldn't tell them what I was planning. My father would never have accepted my saying no to Uncle Sam. With what he'd been through, I understood why. Out of respect and fear, I spared him the grief of trying to explain.

Like most Americans, my mother spent the six o'clock news hour each night with Walter Cronkite. She took note of the daily death toll in Vietnam and worried privately that I'd be added to their ranks. I knew she couldn't oppose my father; neither would it be easy for her to justify my stance to her friends. It was better for the peace of Christmas to not speak about the turmoil that would rise by Easter. I returned to Chico in January, knowing I was facing a decision that would forever alter my life.

22

Dropping Out

IT'S SAID WHEN FACING DEATH, a person's whole life passes in front of them. I experienced it once climbing a Hawaiian cliff above a rising tide. Even with the false sense of invincibility that comes with being nineteen, my life was clearly on shaky ground. A carefree past was being overshadowed by a problem-prone future. Dreams of being a teacher were irrelevant if I didn't finish college. Instead, I'd learn a trade making license plates in prison. It was impossible to stay focused in class studying Western Civilization, when "Real Life 101" was staring at me in the face like no textbook ever did.

I remained on Chico's ski team for the Spring Semester of 1970. The Sierras and their solitude had been a refuge since childhood. The odd bunch of characters on Chico's ski team took my mind off more serious matters. We competed against clubs from Berkeley, Stanford and a host of other Western schools. Races were held around Tahoe, where I was familiar with the terrain and the giant slalom courses we ran. At night around the lodge's fireplace, we'd drink beer and replay the day's events.

One evening, a member of the girls' team became boisterous. She was, as is said about some women, "a little loose to begin with." The more Coors she consumed, the more sordid the tales of her personal life got exposed to the delight of my male companions.

Even though it was the liberated '70's, it troubled me when anyone boasted about their bedroom exploits. Something my grandmother once said caused such conversations to bother me. "When immorality becomes rampant, it will spell the end of the world." Without knowing it at the time, my old Montana relative was chastising the mantra of "free love" that so many in my generation were marching to. I thought the end might be coming for other reasons. But evenings like that around the fire made me think again about her warning. I tried to tune out the drunken female racer. That is, until she got to the topic of my beloved professor.

The alcohol freed her to boast of an affair she claimed to be having with my writing mentor. My teammates found her tale juicy. To me, the news was practically as depressing as hearing my low Lottery number. Not that I was merely sorry for his wife; it did help explain her gloomy demeanor that night in Chico over dinner.

I'd admired him for his intelligence. Now I doubted him because of his character. I had no idea if what Ms. Loose Lips was saying was true. But the bubble I'd built around my professor burst that night in the lodge. Too afraid of the answer to ask him if it was true, I nonetheless took him off the pedestal he'd been the centerpiece of.

When my draft notice finally came that spring, there was no longer a reason to stay in school, or in Chico. Waiting for the day of my pre-induction physical in Oakland, I took off to San Jose where my high school girlfriend was studying. Upon arriving, I learned of her relationship with an older artist. Befitting the period I was in, I chalked the heartbreak up to some odd twist of karma fated to teach me a lesson. Somehow everyone that I had ever been close to would not be there for me during my upcoming Draft ordeal. Along with attempts at self-medication with Lenny Bruce and other banned substances, it was also the time I revisited Herman Hesse.

Reading *Siddhartha* for the first time in Eastern Religions class, it served as a nice primer on Hinduism and Buddhism. Re-reading it in search of meaning, I cast my lot with generations of young seekers who read his books in hopes of finding a key to enlightenment and a doorway out of their youth. Circumstances had stripped me of everyone I believed in and belonged to. Anguish was a constant companion, bringing me along for a ride. Siddhartha's break from the old and embrace of the new spanned a lifetime. I wasn't sure at the time in my life if I had that long to find my way.

Contrary to the advice given by the radical recruitment officer from the SDS, I took the Army physical and passed. I didn't bother trying to convince the U.S. government I was crazy in the short essay that's administered after the exam. Afterwards, I went back to my one-room apartment in San Jose more convinced than ever that my actions were going to land me in jail. Classified 1-A, it was only a matter of weeks before my induction papers would arrive.

23

On the Road

A HIGH SCHOOL FRIEND'S WEDDING in Eugene provided a needed distraction. Greg Keller and I drove up in his red Volkswagen to Oregon, camping as we went. Along the way Greg asked me to be his best man at his upcoming marriage to his high school sweetheart. Given the sad demise of my teenage tryst, I wasn't terribly supportive, but agreed anyway. Since Keller was studying to be a Forest Ranger, he'd figured out a few shortcuts over logging roads guaranteed to get us to Eugene barely in time.

Camping in the middle of the Oregon nowhere, we were welcomed to the evergreen hood by the sound of a far-off wolf. It's funny how safe you feel in a city that's truly treacherous; and how scared you become out in nature with nothing but senseless fears to frighten you to the bone. Leaving Greg to get more firewood, I stayed outside the range of his sight. Just thirty yards away, I could see him as clear as day through the glow of the burning logs. He couldn't see me or detect anything beyond the perimeter of the campfire's flickering flames. I sat still, watching him for the longest time. He fidgeted with the fire and became increasingly uneasy. After about a half hour, he began to call for me. Pat. Pat? Pat! I kept still. Making animal sounds that worried him even more, I finally came back to camp laughing at a pissed-off Greg Keller. The scene of my best friend alone surrounded by a hostile world mirrored how I saw myself. I, too, was upset and on my own, surrounded by an uncertain sphere of darkness everywhere I turned.

The next day we made it to Eugene. Our friend the groom was Dave Jacobsen. We partied like it was 1968 all over again. Poor guy was a roadie for a struggling rock band. Poorer yet, he died while touring from a drug overdose soon after. So did Greg Sears who was a fellow "Mountain Man" who spent a year with us at St. Mary's. In fact, a lot of kids I grew up with at the Lake died from drugs. Hell, even our student body president went to jail for selling the stuff. It was the '70's, and their '60's habits were hard to shake.

I decided to forgo the drive back to California with Greg, figuring the time alone would do me good. Hitchhiking down the Oregon Coast, I brought along a copy of Jack Kerouac's "On the Road." Kerouac ran into a lot of strange cats in his travels. Between the wedding and the coast, I encountered a herd of cows. Unable to get a ride from a rural redneck, I pitched my tent for the evening on a small knoll above a pasture. Waking up the next morning, I was surrounded by a congregation of curious black-and-white dairy cows worshipping at my tent. I ducked back inside, hoping what I'd seen was all a dream! Ten minutes later another peek out, and all of us were still there. My greatest fear was the color of my red tent. Thinking it might incite the inner bull in one of the bovine bystanders, I jumped out of my nylon cavern screaming at the top of my lungs. Being cows, they acted perplexed and hardly moved. They'd probably been expecting a morning hay feed. Disappointed I wasn't the rancher, they wandered off to greener grazing. I kept wandering as well, till my thumb finally caught me a ride to the coast.

There were other lost souls traveling up and down the Oregon coastline. I met up with a bunch of them at Coos Bay. Back then you could sneak past park rangers and camp for the night along the beach. My fellow travelers from the Rainbow Tribe showed how me after building a bonfire out of driftwood, you could sleep all night in toasty sand without the benefit of a blanket. The morning dew proved otherwise and served as my wake-up call. It got me back on the road and away from the sand freaks who tried their best to convert me to their lifestyle.

My next stop was in California below Eureka. A small state park afforded a fire pit and soft grass from which I could sit and ponder Kerouac. Who didn't love his prose? He freed us from convention from commas and from restraints. I also liked the fact, as the Harvard Crimson later eulogized about him, "He couldn't seem to make the transition to the flower-power scene." I was having a hard time with that myself.

I loved how he stayed in desolation on a mountaintop. And though he didn't achieve total enlightenment, he came back down and reported to us what he learned and all he still struggled with. Foregoing knowledge, his pearls of written wisdom came from experiences on the highways of life. I was one of his many dropout disciples on the road, enrolled in Jack's classroom of the fringes.

The evening spent with his book in the Redwoods was perfect. That is, until the midnight deluge began. Springs rains along the Northern California Coast border on the torrential. Thunder and lightning punctuated whatever sleep I got. My one-man pup tent kept me dry for the first couple of hours. After that it surrendered to the forces of nature. Before long my down sleeping bag was nothing more than a sack of wet goose feathers. No nearby shelter to hide under. No car to pile into. No traffic going by to get a lift from. I simply endured the water until it absorbed me, or I it. I became one with the experience and my shivering proved it. I accepted all that the heavens poured down on me. Like my Baptism, it was cleansing something. I just didn't know what. Facing what was coming, I needed plenty of purging. Stormy nights were a precursor of cloudy days. Thank you, Jack Kerouac, for helping clean my soul. Thank you, the rains of April; you prepared me for the storm clouds of May.

As if to give the '60's once last shot at my soul, I stopped by a hippie commune in Sonoma on my way back home. Actually, I was an invited guest of one of the members who picked me up on Highway 101 returning from a foray into the real world on a grocery run. The commune members were huddled in a makeshift camp on forest land owned by an exploitive logging company. Before arriving, my tour guide prepped me on the lack of rules governing the community. And in spite of everyone's best efforts to act laid back and satisfied, they appeared to have the same foibles and inadequacies most from my generation had. Ego and power trips enjoyed their seats around the communal campfire. Relieved to be on my way in the morning, I gave them a contribution toward whatever their cause was, before hitchhiking back to Tahoe.

24

Conscientious Objector

IN TRYING TO RECALL MY FEELINGS about the military and the Vietnam War in 1970, certainly there was an element of fear inside my decision not to go. Not so much fear of jungle warfare against an unbeatable foe, because I would have been naïve enough to believe myself invincible. It was a deep-seated fear arrived at before America's conflict in Southeast Asia; a fear of nuclear war. I remember as if it were yesterday the thirteen days of near panic we felt at home and in the classroom during the 1962 Cuban Missile Crisis. I imagined Vietnam being the tripwire igniting a global nuclear conflict. The image of an erupting mushroom cloud haunted my nineteen-year-old brain.

It's hard to look back forty years and know why you did anything you did at the time. I thought that by not going to Vietnam, I was doing the right thing. I was even willing to suffer the consequences for my convictions. While I thought it was cowardly to run and hide in Canada, I was anything but brave. Still, I tried to be true to myself. However unaware of self I was at the time.

There was one last card to play before the day arrived to "step forward" (or not) at the Oakland Induction Center. It was to apply for Conscientious Objector status and alternative military service. According to government guidelines, to qualify as a conscientious objector, "your lifestyle should consistently reflect the claim you are making." That being the case, I didn't have a snowball's chance in hell of convincing the Selective Service I'd been behaving like Gandhi for the last ten years. Therefore, my attempt at getting a "CO" was wishful thinking at best. But it was thinking I put my heart into. An all-nighter was spent writing twenty-five pages staking out my claim as a peace-loving soul. The thesis was something silly like, "Why God wouldn't want me to kill." Not very original; neither was it persuasive. Unimpressed, my local Draft Board told me to take a hike to Saigon.

The appeal to "someone out there" may not have reached anyone of consequence—but it did strike a chord within me. Even though my faith was mostly non-existent, I was presumptuous enough to write as if I knew God, and what He wanted. Even without a real clue, at least my psychobabble was pointed in the direction of the Almighty. That dark night of my solicitation sent out an SOS that would later elicit a response.

25

Refusing Induction

As ordered, in May of 1970 I reported to Oakland for induction into the U.S. Army. I looked for friends like Randy Koller from the Lake, who'd also refused, to come along for moral support. He had other things to do. In the end, it was better I did what I did alone. There were 250 others in Oakland that day in the same draft boat as me. Black, white, pimpled, and mostly scared-looking, they stood in lines waiting to accept their fate as draftees. After the obligatory introduction to the federal bureaucracy, the only thing left before receiving orders about where to report for duty was the ceremonious moment of being sworn in. We stood in rows, as they would soon be doing in boot camp. The officer in charge read what he was supposed to and the 249 men beside me took the symbolic step forward into the service of the nation. I was the lone soul who didn't.

Noticing that I hadn't joined the others, an officer pulled me out of line and brought me into a back room. I was offered an opportunity to reconsider, and warned that I was in violation of federal law. He told me if my decision was final that I'd be hearing from authorities about a trial date. No threats, no fanfare and no regrets. I did what I came there to do that day in May and left afterward on a lonely Greyhound back to San Jose. It was a long ride for such a short trip.

I now could expect a trial. But I didn't know when. I was sure I'd be going to prison. But I didn't know where or for how long. My life was on hold, but my thoughts were racing and there was no one there to share them with. The SDS hadn't done their job very well. I was the only "resister" that refused induction that day. I assumed their "draftees" simply didn't bother to show up. They were probably running with the beach crowd I met up at Coos Bay.

I was in a veritable demilitarized zone between two warring interests. My only ally was a conscience that felt clear but failed to comfort. I didn't bother calling my parents to tell them what I'd done that day. They'd find out soon enough when the F.B.I. visited to verify my whereabouts.

A lot happened the year I was nineteen. I don't know if it helped me to grow up; but it certainly did age me.

26

Lost in Hawaii

BEFORE GOING BACK TO TAHOE for the summer, I went with a boyhood buddy on a bicycle trip around the Big Island of Hawaii. Visiting nature would be a welcome relief and something I'd not be seeing a lot of if I ended up vacationing at Leavenworth for the next three to five years.

On the flight over from San Francisco Ray Lindsay and I drew up plans to sleep on lush deserted beaches and live off exotic fruits. Upon arriving in Hawaii, the first thing we noticed was the 10,000 or so other mainland kids there pursuing the same pipe dream of paradise. At that time, Hawaii was a new state. It felt like a different country. It was definitely another culture. Native Hawaiians and even local Haoles (white foreigners) resented the influx of American young people trying to live off the excesses of the pineapple fields and the state's welfare system. Their disdain for the two-dollar-a-day unwashed crowd was summed up by one Hawaiian who advised us not to behave like "fruit flies." He reminded us not all of the local Island boys were into peace and love. It was the first, but not the last time I felt like an ugly American in my own country.

My old grammar school friend Ray was an adventurous chap. He'd just finished a backpacking excursion along the Pacific Crest Trail before joining me on our island getaway. Along with his backpack and ten-speed he brought along a severe case of poison oak. It was more-or-less dormant till he reached the equator-like sun of Hawaii. With the ivy reinvigorated, our bicycle trek through the endless plains of the King Cattle Ranch saw Ray bundled up like an arctic explorer. Away from the rains of Hilo, we reached the Kona side of the island where the breeze is constant and the temperatures always warm. Peddling down the coast toward the Island's active volcano, we saw off in the distance a travel-brochure image of a deserted isle. We stashed our bikes and set out through the jungle on a quest for the peace of a black-sand paradise.

Hawaii is blessed not to have snakes. But as Ray can attest, they do have hornets. Leading our way, Ray rousted a colony of the winged avengers. With a cloud of the red dive bombers violently in pursuit, Ray cut a clear swath through the bush. Following at a safe distance, I found him about two miles closer to our final destination in miserable shape. The hornet bites coupled with the aggravated poison oak gave Ray a terrible fever. We figured the best cure would be to camp beneath the lone coconut tree we saw off in the distance. To get there we had to cross a half-moon shaped shoreline with a cliff above the waves too steep to climb. Being from Tahoe and knowing nothing of tides, we set off across the piles of boulders making our way slowly toward the goal. After nearly an hour we were less than half the way there. We both noticed the tide had been steadily rising. Ray and I looked at each other, much like Greg Keller and I did the night the stolen truck was about to get away from us. Between the two of us there was a moment

of unspoken recognition. We'd better get our asses in gear! The survival
instinct kicks in all kinds of glands. Without saying another word, we
made short work of getting to the deserted isle with our lives, if not
our backpacks, intact.

Like all lofty ideals, they appear different once you reach them.
The coconut tree was beautiful; but it was barren. Surrounded by a sea
of blue, there wasn't any fresh water to drink. The black volcanic sand
was luscious but easily swallowed up at night by the Pacific's tides. The
next morning we packed up and hiked back to our bikes. I rode away
thinking picturesque desert beaches are best left alone, or visited only
via postcards.

Ray returned to the mainland to tend his wounds. I went on to
Honolulu to witness the wilds of Waikiki. Traveling, the world is a
small place. Upon arriving I saw a girl I knew from high school and
a guy I'd met at Chico State. She invited me to join her on another
island. He offered me a spot on his apartment floor. Her invitation to
Kauai won out.

I didn't know it at the time, but the woman was pursuing me. Ray
had told her of our itinerary and she flew to Honolulu to rendezvous.
To me it seemed like a coincidence. To her it was an opportunity to
retrieve someone who'd just fallen out of a relationship with an old
high school friend. We flew to the Garden Island. We hiked Kauai's
Waimea Canyon, had dinner together on a veranda and walked along
the beach at sunset. I was happy for the companionship but had too
much on my mind to consider any further emotional entanglements.
I'm sure she expected more. I slept alone that night on the beach. The
next day we sat on the resort's lawn and I told her about my ordeal with
the Draft and everything I was going through. I told her of what hopes
I had for my life after getting out of prison. She predicted I'd one day
run for political office. I joked at her attempt at flattery, remembering

it only after I was elected. We met again thirty years later at our high school reunion. I started to kid her about the time in Kauai, but she didn't have time to talk because she was caring for a dying husband she loved deeply.

My would-be partner went back to Tahoe empty-handed. I returned to Honolulu broke. Besides, I hadn't even set foot on Waikiki's sands or sampled its warm shallow waves. It didn't make any sense to bring the bike, backpack and my plane ticket with me to the beach. I was sure they'd be safe in the vestibule of a nearby neighborhood church. At the beach, I saw my Chico acquaintance. I told him about leaving my belongings in the Lord's house. He gave me his bike and told me to peddle as fast as I could to the church because it was located in what locals called the Jungle Section of Old Waikiki. The "Jungle" was the district where Hawaii's most notorious junkies lived and perused. By the time I returned they'd already lifted my possessions in support of their need. It occurred to me that my faith in the Lord's protection had been misplaced. Then again, drug addicts don't pay close attention to "Thou shalt nots." Counting my blessings, I still had my swim fins, my shorts and the flip-flops I'd worn to the beach. Short of using the fins to paddle cross the Pacific, I wasn't getting back to California in my present state of affairs. At that point, my Chico classmate's offer of his apartment floor was the best thing going.

Wandering around Waikiki one night I met a guy about my age. He was kind enough to invite me up to his place for a glass of wine. We had a pleasant conversation before he sat down on the sofa and put his arm around my shoulder. My first reaction was to unload my sometimes successful right cross before jumping over the sofa and getting the hell out. But something stopped me from striking him. Besides pretending to be a pacifist, I was intrigued to meet a homosexual. I don't think we were calling them gay yet. He seemed surprised that I hadn't been expecting his advances. Describing himself as a bi-sexual, it seemed on the surface to be a contradiction in terms. He told me of his many failed relationships with women and how he found men easier to deal with because they were more like him. Funny, that was exactly why I loved women; they were so much different than men. I left his apartment both relieved and uninitiated. He didn't frighten me, so I guess it can be said I'm not homophobic. However, years later in a Government Affairs Committee in the Nevada Legislature, an off-the-cuff comment I made about an "Adam & Steve nude beach" on Tahoe's East shore caused an openly gay colleague of mine to suspect otherwise.

Under the circumstances, wiring home for money was out of the question. Looking around, I found a job at the Honolulu fish market working for a Portagee named Gomes. His Pig-English was harder for me to understand than the Japanese boat owners who unloaded their fish for me to sort. I left each morning at 4:00 a.m. on a borrowed bike in order to make it the eight miles to the market in time for work. As far as working in a non-English-speaking environment, it didn't matter because all I was doing was sweeping up fish heads, a skill that didn't require a great deal of discourse. After working a week with the constantly angry Gomes, I saved eighty dollars–which was enough in those days for a one-way flight back to California.

27

An Unwelcome Homecoming

AN UNSEASONABLY LATE STORM preceded my return to San Francisco. Thumbing it home to the Lake, an old man in a Plymouth sedan stopped and gave me a ride. He told me he'd never picked up a hitchhiker in his life. Claiming to be clairvoyant, he said he was drawn to me by a voice that told him I was someone special. His purported psychic credentials were verified, he said, by correctly predicting the date of the 1967 Arab-Israeli War. For five hours he explained various "end of the world" scenarios. Having my own theories about what was messing up the planet, we disagreed on most everything. But arguing shortened the trip and kept my mind off the explanation I'd have to give my father for arriving home with next to nothing. Dropping me off at the now-snowing South Shore, he let me out of the car, predicting, "I had a bright and promising future." That was encouraging, because when I entered my parents' house, the prognosis was nowhere near as good.

I'll never forget the look on my Father's face. I faced him shivering in my shorts with a pair of swim fins slung over my back. Yes, it was a freakish snowstorm for early June, but no explanation in the world would have made a father proud of what he saw at his doorstep. Cleaning the snow off my flip-flops, he told me the F.B.I. had been to the house during my absence. It was sad to see my Father so afraid. I couldn't blame him for the scowl or his sentiments. In that uneasy moment, prison would have been preferable to the silence that separated us.

I had no idea when I'd be going to trial. In the meantime, life went on in degrees.

Things were too tense at home to work for my father anymore. Instead, I signed on as a deliveryman for Bonanza Produce, which later purchased the ice business that I wasn't going to take over.

It was also the first summer I tried my fake I.D. at a local casino. My Alabama identity was Bill something-or-other. I spent a fair amount of time rehearsing a Southern drawl in hopes of convincing the security officers at Harrah's that I was indeed a young man from Mobile. Having cashed my first week's paycheck that fateful Friday night, I was about to wish they'd caught me. Within ten minutes, the fruits of my vegetable deliveries belonged to the casino. In that sense, I have Alabama Bill's lost driver's license to thank for curing me of a Nevada habit at an illegally young age.

The summer dragged on and still no word from the Justice Department. Greg got married to his high-school girlfriend. As promised, I served as the best man at their wedding, toasting them to enjoy a life of love. Apparently his wife didn't hear me. A short time later she ran away with Greg's brother-in-law.

Now that I'd dropped out of school, it was awkward hanging around the college party scene. Others spoke of their classes and future careers. I was reduced to explaining an anti-war cause that would soon be enrolling me in jail. Telling people about going to prison got sympathy, but depressed the hell out of anyone long-suffering enough to listen. Whenever possible, I retreated from my predicament deep into Desolation Wilderness, backpacking to fish and forget.

I'd spent all my summers around the Lake. Tahoe permits a person certain amusements on the face of its blue surface. One of the more superficial pleasures is water skiing. Skimming the surface of the indigo blue treasure the Pauites called Ta-hoe brings you only so far. Clutching a nylon rope attached to the sputtering end of an outboard engine struggling to take in air at that altitude doesn't give off the weightless sensation that snow skiing does.

Sailing though is a different story. Gliding across Tahoe's turquoise waters…the blue lady of the Sierras releases her pent-up pleasures. The undulations from her wake-induced waves are like the thighs of a woman in rhythm with the silent lover piercing its keel into her depths. No man-made engine to stroke her, it was nature's raw force delivering you almost to the point of ecstasy. Or something like that.

Inspired by what we saw Hawaiians doing on catamarans and a chance meeting with rock-and-roll sailor David Crosby on his schooner in Sausalito, Ray Lindsay and I decided to buy a sailboat for ourselves. A summer's savings were with us the day we went to purchase a Hobe Catamaran at the local marina. My $500 part of the bargain was tucked safely away in a daypack in the back seat of my Volkswagen. Thinking karma would be served by stopping for a hitchhiker; we picked up a surly looking dude and gave him a ride a few miles down the road to his North Shore rental. Flashing the obligatory peace sign, he departed smiling. Ray and I arrived at the boat shop ten minutes later to put down our deposit. You guessed it. My money was gone.

There were two choices. Since we knew where the thief dude lived, our first option was to go back and beat him to a pulp until he gave the money back. The other was to call the police and enlist their help. Since

I was on record for renouncing violence, we went and told a Placer County Sheriff of the larceny. The circumstantial evidence favored our case. I had the money in the car. We picked up a guy who sat where it was. We dropped him off at his house, and my money was missing. The Sheriff followed us to the thief's place. Cool as a cucumber and grinning like a possum, he denied knowing anything about anything. Despite a record of petty thefts, there wasn't any evidence. Case closed. The cop drove away probably thinking what a dumb ass I was. And he was right. Once again my naiveté purchased an expensive lesson I apparently needed to learn.

Despite the setback, friends pitched in and we got the sailboat. Had I been into reading the scripture at the time, comfort and insight may have been found delving into the life of Job. Loosing everything helped the Old Testament fool strip away some major illusions about life. In my case, I still had a large amount to depart with.

At the end of the summer I decided a sail around the lake would do me good. Tahoe is not as large as one of the Great Lakes, but it has enough in its deep recesses to cover all of California in fourteen inches of water. When evening storms kick up along its West Shore, sails have been known to snap. Ours did one night while out on a warm-up run before the week-long trip. Fortunately, Ray had either a premonition or enough larceny in his veins to save us on that stormy evening. He pocketed a distress beeper from a fellow we were having a beer with at the Sunnyside Bar before setting off on our evening sail. The emergency device came in handy a couple of hours later when a westerly gust broke our mast. The pirated light brought a Coast Guard Cutter to our rescue. With a crippled sail between our pontoons, the catamaran limped home like a shivering dog in tow. We were lucky that night that we didn't have to ride out the storm adrift on Tahoe's chilly waters. With a wounded boat, the voyage around the lake was never made. Probably for the best; it would have been a long soggy trip before that sail was ever furled.

That same year, Richard Nixon was reelected and Henry Kissinger went to Paris to negotiate for peace. The war was far from over, but troop levels were being greatly reduced. The American public had grown weary of the war. Proud wheels in government were turning. Small cogs like me would soon be forgotten. But I didn't know it at the time.

28

In Search of Somewhere

THAT FALL, I WENT SEARCHING FOR A PLACE to get away from it all. Hoping to avoid further turmoil, I dreamed of a big mountain escape. To that end, two pair of skis and what meager belongings would fit were thrown into the black VW.

Jedediah Smith was among the earliest fur hunters to call Wyoming home. Located at a crossroads where trapper trails converged, summers in Jackson Hole in the nineteenth century were the equivalent of a modern-day trade show. Buyers from the Hudson Bay Company came there to trade for pelts. Wilderness lovers far and wide learned of its mountain majesty, helping create the first U.S. National Park at Grand Teton in 1872. Now considered the southern gateway to Yellowstone, Jackson's town square with its four large elk-horn arches has been a gathering spot for American vice presidents, corporate executives and men on the lam from the law.

The resort at Jackson Hole with its 4,000-foot vertical is one bodacious mountain. Only serious ski bums need apply. Arriving in early September, I hooked up with a local hunting guide who took city slickers hoping to bag an antlered wall prize from the nearby National Elk Refuge. Their stuffed heads were shipped off to tongue and groove trophy rooms back in Ohio. The hide of the animal was left with base-camp skinners like me to be stripped from its carcass. The skin and fur of a 1,000-pound bull elk is not to be taken off lightly. I finally had enough the day the local tanner came to collect the hides we'd been storing. We'd been tossing them in a tepee at the edge of camp, which disguised the odor and their hidden contents. The remnants of meat and fat on the back side of the hide are the perfect environment for fly larvae to grow. Told to haul the hides into the tanner's flatbed truck, my ten fingers gushed into thousands of squirming maggots. It was the first time ever walking off a job. I interpreted that close encounter with those soon-to-be flies as a clear sign to move on from Jackson Hole.

A new resort was opening that same year in the Wasatch Range in Utah near old-world ski legend Alta. Called Snowbird by a California dreamer who bought up the mountain's mining claims before making his vision a reality, the resort was desperately trying to open before winter hit. Work could be had with a construction crew digging a communications cable trench from the tramway terminal to the 11,000-foot summit of Hidden Peak. My job was simple. The foreman tossed dynamite in the hole, and grunts like me dealt with the aftermath. Conversations down in a ditch were low-level, dirty and derogatory. The poor foreman who looked and sounded like Richard Nixon took the brunt of our crap. Grumbling and second-guessing the decisions of whoever in the hell was in charge took up most of the day's work.

Employee housing at the resort wasn't yet available, so I moved into a boarding house in Salt Lake with an older mining student from India. The dark-skinned man missed his wife and children terribly.

He'd cry at night talking about them while cooking us lentil curry and boiled eggs on his hot plate. I'd listen to his sad refrain before falling asleep from the day's toils. By then we were working twelve-hour-a-day shifts trying to connect the cable before the snows fell. It was the Honolulu fish market all over again. I'd leave for work before sunup and get back home when it was down. At least this time I was shoveling rocks and not Red Snapper heads.

Snowbird opened late that first season because of problems with the tram and the threat of avalanches. Hired on as a bellman and part-time night manager at the Lodge, the days were mine to ski for free. A rollaway bed in a pitch-black linen closet served as a temporary home. That way, when a storm closed the canyon, there was no missing a good powder day in Peruvian Gulch. Being a certified instructor, the resort used me to ski with VIP guests on back-country helicopter trips. Little Cottonwood Canyon's endless powder fields attracted plenty of skiing purists. Bobby Kennedy's kids were among those I guided down Snowbird's virgin slopes that inaugural year.

The first day Snowbird opened to the public, a local college student was buried alive in the resort's first avalanche. The Ski Patrol gathered everyone in sight and gave us aluminum poles to probe for the lost and freezing soul. Locked arm-in-arm, we walked down the path of the slide, finding no trace of the missing skier. After another try, someone's probe hit a hard object. Being buried in three feet of snow had turned the BYU freshman purple enough to audition for the California Raisins. He stood up praising the Lord and hugging everyone he could. Along with the hand of the Divine, his own strong arm had kept him alive. Before passing out, he managed to dig an air pocket around his mouth. He was lucky it wasn't Tahoe's "Sierra Cement" that buried him that day. Utah's light powder was porous enough to give him enough oxygen to survive. Blankets and hot cocoa took away the hypothermia. Recovering, he told how he'd heard the line of rescuers pass over the first time with no success. He yelled, but no one heard. Giving himself up for dead, he blacked out until he was resurrected by the sharp jab of his savior's pole.

I've witnessed my share of "salvations" since that day on the slope, but I've never seen someone reborn with the same unbridled joy as was seen on his face. Snowbird wisely bestowed its own version of amazing grace by giving him a free season pass, thus avoiding a public-relations disaster on their first day of operations.

Ski bumming is an art form. Only the young have the gumption to pull it off and make it to the real world beyond. If someone's still hanging around a ski area in their thirties, they're not going far in life beyond the slopes. There were a few such aging creatures to be found at Snowbird. Most were college students taking time off school because they'd either flunked out their first year, their parents had a messy divorce or they were struck by a strange wanderlust like Dorothy of Oz that deposited them in the middle of the West's mountains looking for the yellow brick road to skiing bliss.

There was Charley from Wisconsin who worked as a cook and played guitar and sang like Neil Young. Beth and Lisa exchanged classes at Dartmouth for scrubbing bathrooms in the Lodge. Greg was a lanky engineering student from the University of Michigan who knew he'd be in school for the next six years and decided to have fun in between. A former mayor of New York's younger brother was enjoying his trust fund, not having to work like the rest of us. There was red-haired Anne, a struggling art student from Seattle who had no clue why she was there. George and Linda, a husband-and-wife team, worked as Lodge managers before returning to their life on Wall Street. I met Linda in Manhattan when I was doing Church fundraising for UNICEF. Seeing me on a 5th Avenue bus, she burst into tears remembering that year in Utah when mountain serenity replaced the rat race.

My favorite fellow bum was Bob Goodman. From a good Mormon family in Moscow, Idaho, he too was on the lam. Not from the law, but from going on his LDS mission abroad. I suppose he was considered a "Jack" Mormon by some of his church elders. But to me, he was a saint in the most secular of settings. Of all the countless testimonials and blue *Books of Mormon* I received from Utah believers, my friend from Idaho was by far the best witness to his faith. His pure heart was more easily understood than the story of Moroni, some sort of glorified and resurrected being in the religion.

29

Deep in the Canyon

THE SKI SEASON CAME TO AN END with sunshine, corn snow and an illegal plunge into the guest swimming pool. Once the snows melted, kids returned to their homes in the Midwest. Goodman and I headed for the Grand Canyon in his 1968 foam-insulated yellow convertible Volkswagen bus that later became mine. Our goal was to get to the South Rim of the Canyon before the tourists did. Stuffing all the dry foods we could fit into our backpacks, we hiked down the dusty switchbacks carved by decades of wear from bands of Indians, grizzled prospectors on burrows and fellow thrill seekers like ourselves.

Crossing the immense gorge cut by the Colorado River, we encountered marvels of the human variety that complemented nature's grand ones. There was the 48-year-old machine tool salesman from Chicago determined to make the trek across the canyon before he died. Given his weight and how exhausted he appeared, I'm not sure he got his wish. We met an elderly couple counting every step it took to walk from one rim of the canyon to the other. They wouldn't tell me why they were counting. That secret was reserved for their grandchildren.

One evening after dinner, I sat on a sandstone ledge and watched a thunderstorm gather over the North Rim. Before long lightning triggered a blaze in a far-off patch of forest pasted to a craggy cliff. A weather system away, the fire was no more than a passing fancy in the splendid scheme of nature. Against the panorama of the grandest of nature's canyons, the isolated incident helped me put certain matters in perspective. Like flying over a small town at 10,000 feet, there's an order and peace not seen from the streets below. Before me a fire burnt out of control in one corner of the globe. Even so, it failed to disturb the tranquility of the whole. As a consequence of that moment, my Draft travails seemed small in comparison. Feeling like a winning ticket holder on the prize of planet earth, qualms about the future dissipated with the rains. A momentary realization of life in its fullness flirted with me that night in the canyon. But like all teases, only the memory remained after the brush with beauty was gone. Still, if somewhere the "bigger picture" can be found, the Grand Canyon is a good place to go looking for it.

Reaching the mighty Colorado, a narrow suspension bridge crosses the boiling caldron on its way to light the Vegas Strip. Clinging to the shaky planks over the river with Nature's most deafening sound, we saw three rubber rafts of soaked-and-screaming adventurers shooting the rapids below us. There's a fine line between exhilaration and terror. It wasn't clear what side these paying customers were on. The reward for our making it over the suspension bridge was a Snicker's Bar that was every bit as magnificent as the ice-cold waterfall we found to shower under on the way up to the North Rim. Traversing roundabouts with forty-pound backpacks does wonders for the appetite. Before finishing half the journey, we'd eaten most of our dehydrated dinners.

Given my canyon catharsis, a guardian angel provided assistance in the form of South Tahoe's Homecoming Queen. Arriving at one of the few campsites along the Canyon's narrow switchbacks, we ran into Phyllis Jones and her new husband. His name and rank were insignificant in the presence of Phyllis. She was every bit as lovely looking and regal in a tank top and cutoffs as she was that day at the football game in 1968 in her pink chiffon dress and seated on the back of Brad Lampson's yellow Corvette. Despite his reservations, Phyllis persuaded her husband to share some of their food with us. I never saw her again after that night in the Grand Canyon. I learned she later divorced the stingy spouse. The funny thing was, I did run into him again. After they separated, he found his way, like me, to the Unification Church. He was managing a Church-owned jewelry store in Chicago when I became his pastor. He barely remembered our chance encounter. And despite all the Church taught about unselfishness, he was as tightfisted with tithing as he was with his packaged beef stroganoff that night on the trail.

We made it to the top of the North Rim and like basketball practice doing a "U.C.L.A. drill," we immediately turned around and retraced our steps back to the South Rim to find the tourists had arrived in droves. Two things made for such a hasty return, the approach of Mother's Day and the lump in our stomachs. Bob, being the perfect son that he was, wanted to make it to a pay phone by Sunday morning to wish his Mom a happy holiday. I put it in gear, knowing my mother, too, would love a call from her wayfaring stranger. The other reason we motored up the switchbacks at breakneck speed was the simple motivating fact…we were out of food.

I've since fasted on numerous occasions for seven days at a time for the purpose of spiritual purification and paying a price for my sins. Forced fasting or starving to death, as it occurred to us at the time, was far more difficult. The round trip took a week; which means we couldn't have gone without food for more than two or three days. But not knowing where our next meal was coming from made it seem like forever.

We got up to the South Rim on Sunday morning in time to call our mothers. Bob's devotion to Mom and apple pie didn't go unrewarded. After dutifully phoning home collect, we splurged on Americana's famous dessert with ice cream, along with as many Coke's and hot dogs our pooled thirty-five dollars could purchase at the tribal campground store. Indigestion was worth the price of recovery from the self-imposed famine. At least that was the way we saw it at twenty-one years of age having just conquered the Grand Canyon.

30

End of the Road

AFTER THE TRIP, Bob returned home to his family in Idaho. I hope they forgave him for not going on his church mission to Uruguay. He's the only Mormon I ever knew who never tried to give me the Blue Book. And yet, he was a living testimony to the goodness his church background seemingly instilled in him. Before returning home, Bob sold me his yellow convertible VW Bus with the portals and the sprayed-on Styrofoam insulation. It was a flower child's dream come true. The problem was, I wasn't much of a hippie to begin with. But I did bring along a young blonde thing I'd met skiing at Snowbird who *thought she was.*

She left home in Southern California to join the Volkswagen and me on a journey to God knows where. Not yet healed from my last romantic go-around, I nonetheless took off with a nineteen-year-old girl on a trip through the Canadian Rockies. She was star struck by the experience and had no idea how emotionally broken I still was. Thinking about my future one day driving west from Banff, I pictured myself ending up an old man, hat on my lap, staring out from the lobby of a gentleman's hotel. A telephone call and an apology to her mother preceded the purchase of a one-way ticket back to Riverside for my blue-eyed traveling companion.

During my drive back to Tahoe, the VW broke down in Idaho. Being over-zealous and under-qualified to fix the problem, I attempted to decipher the simpleton's diagrams from *The Idiot's Guide to Volkswagen Repair*. After three days on the side of the highway with no self-repair in sight, I hitched a ride to the nearest town and got a tow.

Eating dry packaged pancakes minus syrup and being dive-bombed by carnivorous gnats was a sure recipe for missing my mother's cooking and her warm embrace. Weary from life on the road, I returned to Tahoe to rest and recover. Traveling, the universal remedy for my generation, had lost its appeal. The realization that brought an end to my journeys was that wherever I went to get away, I brought myself along for the ride. The question was no longer where to go, but what to become?

Like Forest Gump, I'd reached the end of my run.

31

My Own Life Had "Restoration Project" Written All Over It

By 1972, THE VIETNAM WAR had fallen into disfavor with enough of the American public to bring it to an end. Nixon visited China, signaling a change in Pacific strategies. The first Watergate arrests took place and by the end of the year there were only 24,000 American troops left serving in Southeast Asia. Draft resisters like me soon became an afterthought to Washington. In the end, I was among the 360,000 who were never formally charged. When all the war angst was over and done with, I never stepped inside a prison—except for the one of my own making.

The yellow VW and I limped home to Tahoe. In spite of my prodigal past, my folks did what good parents do. They took me back.

An Indian summer was spent restoring the Gold Hill Hotel and Saloon, just below Twain's Virginia City. The owners had lost an adventurous son to a motorcycle accident. I filled in as a sad reminder as they tried to put the building and their lives back together. My own life had "restoration project" written all over it. Sifting sand looking for old square nails from the Comstock Era paralleled my own search for what was missing and what could be found.

There was plenty to mend in the relationship with my parents. It was as hard as ever for them to accept all I'd put them through. Still, they were happy to have me home. I accepted their authority, with curfews and restrictions like high school all over again. An attempt was even made to enjoy network television with them after Mom's dinners of my favorite childhood meals. But like any stay in the hospital, the time at home was no more than a temporary stay. Neither party knew the prognosis for my recovery. In the end, parental care can only do so much for someone society says should be an adult. After a few passing months of teaching skiing at Heavenly and living at home; a different kind of longing set in.

Father Grace and the Catholic Church were still around. So, too, were my questions. Reading Far Eastern philosophies occupied quiet nights after game-show viewing with the folks. Eastern thought was intellectually stimulating but left me emotionally empty. The idea of detachment from the material world was fine on one level, but it didn't leave a lot to live for here on earth. At twenty-two, I didn't know which way to go—but I was heading there regardless.

32

A Different Path

MONTANA MEANT A NEW BEGINNING. The place where my Mother's parents were from represented their past and my future. For the present, I made plans to work there in order to gain residence and finish college. An old family friend from Heavenly Valley was the mountain manager for retired NBC broadcaster Chet Huntley's new resort, Big Sky. Employment in the ski industry could be found until I became a Montanan and could afford to register for school.

The yellow VW van was bequeathed to an aspiring road warrior. Farewell to my parents seemed eerily final. Receiving their reluctant blessing, I took none of their cash. Leaving home felt like it was for good. At least I hoped so.

I headed east on America's "Loneliest Road" (U.S. Highway 50). Driving the 500 miles across Nevada's barren desert landscapes at night could have passed for another planet. Barren Mars-like peaks stood propped against an endless starlit sky. Doing an all-nighter to Salt Lake felt like leaving the world as I knew it. Montana symbolized a change hoped for and the start to a chapter not yet written. Before arriving anew in Montana, something old was still waiting in Utah.

Being mid-April, spring skiing lingered at Snowbird. Revisiting my previous haunt meant staying with an engineer friend who helped owners' Ted Johnson and Dick Bass design the area's massive tramway. It so happened, that Japanese adventurer Yuichiro Miura was visiting Ted for the week. Miura's heroics included a Kamikaze-like schuss down Mt. Fuji followed by a near-fatal attempt to ski down Mt. Everest. A parachute saved the daredevil from sliding off a 6,000-foot ledge on the Himalayan giant. His latest endeavor was to partner with Johnson to build a new ski resort in Sapporo, the sight of the recent winter Olympic Games. After a day of helicopter skiing with the two men, Miura surprised me with an invitation to go to Japan to serve as an advisor to the new area's ski school. Thrilled at the prospect of going abroad, I thought, "Why not?"

Getting to sleep that night was hard mulling over whatever odd fortune it was that was giving me an all-expense-paid trip to Japan. Serendipity, it seemed, had visited in the form of an audacious stranger from the Far East. Before falling asleep, I had every intention of taking Mr. Miura up on his offer. That is, until my grandparents appeared to me in a dream.

More like a visitation than a dream—the both of them stood at the end of my bed and pleaded with me to go on to Montana. Waking up early the next morning, I couldn't put the encounter with my deceased relatives out of my mind. Breakfast was scheduled with Mr. Miura to finalize details for the visit to Japan. There was no rationale for refusing. No reasonable explanation for any second thoughts. It was an offer too good to be true. And I was going to pass on it. Not knowing what to say, I packed my bags in the morning and drove down Little Cottonwood Canyon without a word. My grandparents' ephemeral plea won over Miura's worldly enticement. It was now a matter of seeing where the dream would lead. A few days after, I called my engineer friend and tried to explain. He thought I was crazy.

On the road to Montana, I replayed over and over in my mind the image of my grandparents' appearance. Finally reaching the narrow canyon that borders Big Sky, the road cleared to reveal the same kind of huge Western resort I'd worked at in Wyoming and Utah. Magnificent as it was, the mystique was no longer in the mountain—but in what lay beyond.

Bozeman is a sleepy college town sandwiched in between Big Sky Country's western mountain ranges and her vast eastern plains. A visit to Montana State University was the first order of business. While checking out residency requirements, a flyer on a campus bulletin board caught my eye and stopped me dead in my tracks. It read: "Did Jesus really come to die?" Flashing back to my Good Friday moment in the pew at St. Theresa's, I remembered asking the same question when I was sixteen.

33

New Answers to Old Questions

A EUROPEAN-LOOKING FELLOW, identified by the strange tennis shoes he wore, eyeballed me as I stood there reading the bulletin. Introducing himself as Morti from Finland, he told me he was from the One World Crusade, the program's sponsor. Reassuring him I'd be there later that afternoon for the lecture, he appeared genuinely surprised when I actually showed up. Later he confided he didn't think someone as "worldly looking" as myself would have much interest in the subject matter. Little did he know.

The lecturer was a rosy-cheeked German woman by the name of Christine. She gave an intriguing talk about God and the universe. The brown-haired woman's thick accent couldn't contain her enthusiasm for the subject. The lecture presented ideas that seemed both familiar and new. It was as if I was hearing something I knew deep down–but had never heard before.

The Divine Principle described the universe as the effect of a loving first cause. God and human beings were compared to a mind and body;

one the internal character, the other the external form. Masculinity and femininity reflect the Creator's original nature and are embodied in image form in all of life from basic particles to the first human parents. Pairs throughout nature were meant to complement and complete each other. The goal of creation was incarnation; God seeing Himself in us; we becoming our true selves in Him. Jesus said as much. Some believe he was as much. What thrilled me was the possibility that we all could be as much.

Another attendee, an aging leftist organizer on campus, kept interrupting Christine's presentation. Not there to listen, he parroted old Marxist axioms like "religion being the opium of the people." Having already heard that argument from my communist professors in Chico, I was interested in hearing a new point of view and told him so. The two of us got into a shouting match before he left in a revolutionary huff.

Following the talk, the members seemed genuinely interested in what I thought. The skeptic in me warned that any group expression of sincerity might be a technique meant to entice. But with the dream of my grandparents still fresh in my mind, I checked my skepticism at the door. The invitation to visit their home the following evening to hear a second presentation was gratefully accepted.

Despite fresh powder the next day up at nearby Bridger Bowl, I easily lost interest in skiing. Sitting in the lodge pondering the previous night's presentation, it seemed as if what the Grateful Dead sang was true, and "what a long strange trip" it had been. The Draft ordeal, my failed relationships, the endless search for answers coupled with the dream of my grandparents...all seemed to be converging at this point in my life. The question now was whether this small group of Europeans and whatever was behind them was the reason I had come to Bozeman?

Visiting their tiny off-campus apartment that next night, it was immaculately clean and minus any furniture save for the solitary rocking chair left by the previous tenant. My mother had taught never to go to someone's home for a meal empty-handed. My companion for dinner was a fresh peach pie purchased at the last minute from a local farmer's market. Later, the members said they believed the baked offering was an important condition for my awakening. I figured it was just being polite.

Dinner was served on the floor, Indian-style, seated around a plastic Italian tablecloth. The meal was a simple casserole comprised of everything that hadn't been consumed the night before. An electric atmosphere rendered the humble cuisine unimportant. Table talk, minus the table, flowed without pretense or the assistance of any adult beverages or banned substances. Compared to the bohemians and ski bums I'd been accustomed to socializing with, there was an openness and contentment within this bunch that not even the coolest crowd I'd hung with had ever come close to exhibiting.

Listening to the second evening's lecture on the Fall of Man, the implications were staggering. The original separation from the Creator stemmed from the pair on the ground—and not some apple in a tree. No test of faith from the Almighty, the first humans' fall from grace was, sadly, a human affair. Instead of sexual love making the first couple into parents resembling God, their premature union resulted in emotional baggage and bad parenting that produced brother-on-brother violence and humanity's first dysfunctional family. No rap lyrics, shock jocks or the Exxon Valdez oil spill tainted the atmosphere of early Eden. Paradise was lost when humanity's early parents discovered their sexuality before they found themselves.

Found were reasons for my own failures in relationships. I saw my parents' problems, my grandparents' plight and a host of humanity's ills from a wholly different perspective. Heck, it even got me thinking about forgiving Richard Nixon; realizing he too was the product of imperfect parenting. Actually, I wasn't that far along in my redemption; but the thought crossed my mind of forgiving *Tricky Dick* in that moment of fleeting enlightenment.

Most of my life I'd wondered about the person of Jesus. The next lecture filled in the theological blanks that had been hotly debated during the late night dorm sessions at St. Mary's. Jesus was a man who fulfilled his Divine potential. Not God. Not both. When the lecture finished, I sat there and thought to myself; Jesus the man, who became like God, was more compelling than Christ the God, who became like man. It was the beginning of my hope and the start of my transformation.

After almost a week of coming back each evening to hear a different talk, I was set to hear the conclusion in a presentation entitled "The Second Coming of Christ." Sensing the anticipation members had for me in hearing the conclusion, I told them I understood intellectually what they were teaching–but I didn't feel emotionally what I saw in their faces.

That was about to change.

Critics of the Unification Church, which I didn't know existed in 1973 – the critics or the Church–have labeled its conversion methods a form of brainwashing. It's been an effective stigma that has worked to the advantage of the Movement's detractors, especially given the founder's country of origin.

Faith for most converts is arrived at by more than mere logic and reason. It took the blinding light experience of Jesus appearing to Saul on the road to Damascus to knock the former Jew off his high horse and change his outlook on the man from Nazareth. That clear cold night in Bozeman, I was about to have an experience that would knock the proverbial socks off my searching soul.

After dinner, I overheard a discussion between Christine Redmond, my German teacher, and Robin Kuhl, the English-center director. She confided to him her insecurities about delivering the final talk. It seemed the state leader who normally taught the lectures was away at a conference in New York with the Teacher. They argued about whether or not it would be wiser to wait for his return to deliver the final presentation to me and the few other guests who'd been studying the Principle. I was relieved when they decided to go ahead and teach what I'd come to hear. At that point, I wasn't interested in toastmaster professionalism, but whether or not Christ had returned to the earth!

It was decided that since Christine wasn't confident in presenting the material, she would instead read from the final chapter of Dr. Young Oon Kim's book, *The Divine Principles*. A professor of New Testament and Comparative Religion at Ewha University in Seoul, Ms. Kim wrote the first English translation of the "heresy" that resulted in her being banned from the prestigious women's Methodist institution in Korea.

Sitting on the floor of the plain upstairs bedroom, Christine began reading from the final chapter on the "Second Advent of the Messiah." Reviewing how the Reformation and the Renaissance had prepared the religious and scientific environments for the Second Coming…a strange feeling began to come over me.

At that point in the evening something happened I'd never experienced before, or since. While she was reading, the room turned a golden haze. At the same time an unusual calm came over me, filling my every sense. Rather than hearing the familiar sound of Christine, a voice from somewhere inside began quietly explaining how, when and where the messiah would return. To this day, no one has been able to tell me what took place in those fifteen-or-so minutes suspended in time. Sitting there afterwards pondering what had happened, it seemed that God had spoken to me.

Curious why such an astonishing revelation about Christ's return would be given to someone as worldly as me, I couldn't help but think of the starry surprise the shepherds witnessed in Bethlehem the night Jesus was born. When the talk was over, I sat there pondering my apparent good fortune. Afterward, I asked a guest seated beside me if she'd heard the "voice?" She said "no." And left the Center grumbling about Christine's German accent and how hard it was to understand much of anything that was taught.

The lecture foretold that Christ would return to earth, not on the clouds, but in the same way he came 2,000 years ago, as a man. The chosen nation would not be Israel this time, but a Pacific Rim country. At that point–my mind raced ahead. What Eastern sages did I know that might qualify as the coming Asian avatar? Given my previous Leftist political leanings, I wondered if either Mao Tse-tung or Ho Chi Minh might be a candidate for the Second Coming of Christ. Good thing neither of them was. I certainly didn't need the Federal Government taking a renewed interest in my case because I was following an avowed enemy of the United States. I had just encountered an adventurous Japanese visionary in the form of Mr. Miura in Utah. But I figured if some higher power had wanted me to follow him, I'd now be having Sake in Sapporo instead of heeding the dream that deposited me in Montana. I had no idea who the new messiah might be. No mention was made of Sun Myung Moon. I wouldn't have known the name if he had been proclaimed.

Another thing happened that bright spring eve in Bozeman that sealed my fate as a disciple. While trying to digest whatever was my mystical experience, I took a walk outside alone along a nearby deserted railroad track. It was cold as only Montana can be on a clear April night. Strangely still warm within from my close encounter with the voice, I came upon a divide in the tracks and off in the distance saw a dark figure tending a campfire along the embankment to the left. Following the crumbling tracks toward the light, I felt the strongest urge to join the distant stranger. Then suddenly a chill interrupted my pace. Thinking the figure, real or imaginary, represented a return to my old life, I turned around and walked back to the Center believing it was time to begin a new one.

The members were waiting at the door and embraced me. I was the first "man" to join the Movement in Montana; if you could call someone twenty-two years of age and feeling like a child on the verge of taking his first steps, a man. The first thing I said as I entered their world was that now I felt what they felt, but didn't understand what they believed. That would change as I studied the Principle whenever I could and one day became a national lecturer for the Church.

34

Shorter On Hair But Longer on Humility

A VISIBLE MANIFESTATION OF THE CHANGE taking place was for me to get a haircut. Or at least that was what a German "older brother" told me the day after joining. Going to do so was the first test of my newborn faith. Borrowing a bike for the trip to get my ears lowered, I peddled furiously the entire way resenting being told what to do. Bringing along a poor attitude to the barbershop got me a bad haircut in return. Lesson learned. The law of cause and effect did work. Sufficiently shorn, I returned shorter on hair but longer on humility.

One of things that perturbed parents about Reverend Moon in those early days was that he got kids to do things they wouldn't do for their own parents. Getting their hair cut, dressing conservatively and saying no to drugs– and doing it for Reverend Moon—was an affront to their parental authority.

Ironically, my beleaguered parents ended up seeing him before I did. Agitated by a steady stream of surprisingly righteous letters about the great new truth and teacher I'd found, they decided to check out the man and his message at a public speech the Reverend was giving in Berkeley. Puzzled by the fact that his talk was punctuated by a guttural Korean dialect requiring the use of an interpreter, they also weren't happy that his sermon was about ten times longer than any one they'd ever heard from Father Grace. They were impressed by the young folks they met. Struck by the members' kindness and their conservative appearance, my Mom and Dad were pleased with the fruit of what they saw. But like most Americans, they would soon become worried about the unusual Far Eastern tree that was producing it.

35

On the Way to Heaven

ON MY WAY TO HEAVEN, I put my parents through hell. In the span of just three years…I'd dropped out of college, refused induction into the Army, and traipsed through Canada in a hippie van headed nowhere. Culminating my departure from the mainstream was the joining of a new religious movement that most would soon consider a cult. It was a lot for my middle-of-the-road American folks to digest. Even though I wouldn't change what happened, it took decades and having my own children to fully appreciate what I put them through as parents.

Whatever it was that had gotten into me from that moment I heard the "voice" hadn't yet worked its way out of my system. Anxious to tell anyone I could that Christ had returned to the earth, I met a young woman recruiting for the Peace Corp on campus. Accepting my invitation to attend an introductory lecture that evening at the Center, she came accompanied with her own agenda hoping to find dreamers interested in devoting two years of their post-college life in some far off place like the Congo.

Thrilled to learn she too was a Catholic, I invited the young woman to return the next night to hear the second part of the revelation that was revolutionizing my life. She declined, explaining she already had a mission in Missoula the next day seeking volunteers for Sargent Shriver's organization. Taken aback that she wasn't floored by the same knowledge that was mesmerizing me, I nonetheless convinced her to sit long enough in the lounge of the women's dorm for me to unload on her everything I knew about Christ's return. Believing she'd drop her Peace Corp career like St. Peter did his fishing nets, after a couple of hours she excused herself from my impassioned clutches and bid me a polite farewell.

Her rejection left me stunned. Sad beyond my prior human heartbreaks, I walked out into the dimly lit campus courtyard when suddenly the spring buds on the trees glistened and turned gold—just as the lecture room had. A white-bearded figure appeared to my right saying he was Paul. Not sure how to deal with a visit from a 2,000-year-old apostle, I was too afraid to look him in the eye. He told me we had something in common. We did? Was I too a persecutor of Christ like Saul had been before he became Paul? At the moment I remembered putting down kids from California who'd become Jesus freaks and the all demeaning things I'd said about Billy Graham and others when I heard Christianity was making a comeback on college campuses. Leaving the courtyard, the trees stopped their flickering and Jesus' disciple left me to my own conclusions about my future as a follower. Returning to the Center that night felt like coming back home. It would be decades before I ever considered leaving.

"Spiritual experiences" like I had were not uncommon among members in the early days of the Church. Was it because there was so little "physical" foundation and those in the spiritual world were active in lieu of no earthly vehicle to proclaim a great new truth? Was it that way with Jesus when so many early testimonies to him were from those who were spiritually open to some higher voice? I don't know. The fact that noticeably less of that sort of thing is happening in Unification circles today to draw people through dreams and revelations may also mean something. Now 35 years later, "Doubting Thomas" might be the disciple who visits me, saying what we have in common is the search for "proof" that the new messiah is all that he is believed to be.

In the early days of the American Movement, not everyone heard voices or had grandparents and apostles appear to them like I did. Many, like my Peace Corp contact, continued on their own way to find the first Christ or no Christ at all.

In the months spent in Bozeman and Missoula in the early 1970's, a number of young Americans did join me in the cause. There was Alex Colvin, a wandering troubadour from California whom I taught the Principle and argued with for hours on end before a light went off in his head and he turned to writing his tunes in praise of the new Christ. There was Joe Godwin, a potter from New Hampshire who heard a voice through me like I did through Christine. Joe made it all the way to the Founder's estate in Tarrytown where he worked as an artist in residence before he left with his pottery and the Korean wife Reverend Moon gave him. And there was Rob Sayre, who worked as a mechanic at a truck stop in Missoula and lived downstairs from us. Rob would never come to a lecture when invited. But he did come upstairs when I asked him to fix the plumbing. His willingness to help others was the hook that got him to join. Rob continues doing good deeds like running a publishing house, having a blessed family and serving others before he does himself.

Crossing over from the secular to the sacred wasn't easy for a person like me. Some days I'd sneak down to the basement coveting my burgundy Rosignol skis– imagining a downhill schuss back to a life requiring far less sacrifice of self.

Fundraising was a staple of life in the early days of the Church. One thing for sure, asking for donations either scares or humbles the hell out of you. Francis of Assisi's followers, Buddhist monks and the bell-ringers from the Salvation Army have all been through it. As the Good Book says, there were benefits for both the giver and the receiver. Remembering that Jesus taught anyone giving even "a cup of water in my name will not lose his reward," fundraising was an opportunity to be blessed with a multitude of unusual experiences. It took character, and sometimes being one, to get a person to give. Developing a deep heart, a paramount virtue for any Unificationist, was aided by the rejection routinely faced when asking folks to depart with their hard-earned dollars.

Going door-to-door could be risky in rural Montana. It was a chance to be bitten by a cow dog, shot at by an angry protectionist when you missed seeing his "survivors will be prosecuted" sign, or being severely judged by a righteous believer because, whatever it was you were peddling, it had to be of the devil. In fact, only a fervently religious person would stop and thank God after being bitten by a dog, as I once did while selling candles in Kalispell. Believing that praising His name was preferable to using it in vain (as I was formerly inclined to do), I thanked God while tending to the puncture of my Achilles heel for the opportunity to pay for a past life of sin.

There was the time in New York selling flowers in front of Grand Central Station in the middle of a frigid New Easterner, when a lady of the night approached a middle-aged commuter on his way home from a late night at the office. Her proposition was being seriously entertained until I intervened with the chance for him to buy a flower to "help keep families together." My presence reminded him of someone waiting at home and he shuffled off nervously to catch his train. It also alerted the streetwalker's pimp of the trick I'd just cost them. Chasing me down 42nd Street in high heels with purse flailing on the back of my head, I felt strangely righteous like the first time I served Mass at St. Teresa's. Times like that helped you "find a friend in Jesus," and made for good stories to swap at testimony time.

Before being sent off to New York to meet Reverend Moon and prepare for his 1974 speaking engagement at Madison Square Garden, I spent a final weekend in nature in God's first Bible. A Church director from Seattle visited Missoula to shepherd our small flock in the Montana outback. In celebration of my going off to Manhattan as the state's first missionary, Regis Hanna took the group on a weekend outing near Glacier Park–a place that truly is God's country. Taking a day-long hike to a mountain ridge overlooking an alpine lake, I saw my old life in a new place. In the distance was a small village that reminded me of parts of Tahoe. Making it to the edge of a windy peak, we viewed the sun setting over the world to the west. Rising over our shoulders to the east, the moon came up behind us. Symbolic or not of the ascension of the Reverend, the evening ended with prayers and songs atop the ridge. Whether we were perched between the sunset of an old age and the dawn of a new…remains to be seen. But that day's mountaintop experience left me believing we were.

36

Wilderness of the 20th Century

CRITICS OF THE UNIFICATION CHURCH in the early days accused it of getting its converts to give all their possessions over to the man and his movement. In my case it was true, but they didn't get much. I pawned my skis for the one-way plane ticket to New York and bequeathed my beat-up black VW to the local members. At the time, donating my meager belongings symbolized a break with my past and seemed a small offering in exchange for the chance to build the Kingdom.

Flying for the first time east of the Rockies, America is a different place. From a window seat compliments of the Friendly Skies, the endless squares of farmland and the orderliness of Midwestern towns is a far cry from the jagged mountain spires that are the West. Past midnight, my missionary flight descended over Manhattan. Gliding past the Empire State Building robed in its nightly red, white and blue spot-lighted vests, the towering symbol of New York seemed close enough to touch. I didn't know it at the time, but I'd soon be hawking my new beliefs beneath its midday shadows.

The dreamer in me half expected the Church to welcome me with a ticker-tape parade down 5th Avenue. Instead, I arrived minus any fanfare and barely enough bus fare to get me to the East 71st Street Center near Central Park. At such an ungodly hour, this sleepy country bumpkin from Bozeman was in for a somber awakening. His name was Joe Tully. The young Center director wasn't tickled with the sound of a buzzing doorbell at 3:00 a.m. on that cold autumn morning. Members from America's hinterlands had been arriving in advance of Reverend Moon's upcoming speech at Madison Square Garden. Joe had been run ragged housing and deploying the troops for the upcoming campaign. Certainly no ticker-tape parades were planned by Mr. Tully, who looked and acted like the boot-camp sergeant I'd have gotten had I gone along with the Army's plans for me. Joe, a Stanford grad and friend of golfer Tom Watson, didn't suffer fools and was either deadly serious or deathly tired the night he greeted me at the doorstep of the brownstone the Church leased on New York's Upper East Side. This was the same Joe Tully who, some thirty-three years later after a series of heart surgeries and the loss of a wife he adored to cancer, was there on my land in the Sierras trying to gingerly revive a Rainbow Trout he'd caught before releasing it back into the Little Walker.

Then, Joe took me to the basement cafeteria where I was introduced to my first of many cucumber-and-mayonnaise sandwiches. The Japanese missionary sisters who'd commandeered the kitchen were still learning the art of American sandwich-making and what ingredients should apply. Olive-and-cheese sandwiches were another of their mysterious concoctions. Such gastronomical offerings were as ill-conceived as an American making a sushi hand roll with peanut butter and jelly. But since the Movement stood for the unifying of religions and races; the mixing of recipes was as good a place as any to start.

Following the stranger-than-any-munchies midnight snack, Joe sent me to join Wesley Samuels, who was doing his late-night janitorial duties at a private school across the street. Wesley worked at nights making money to support a wife and children because he offered his days to God for free. My introduction to the Messiah's work on that first night in Manhattan was mopping floors; which was probably about what I would have been doing had I joined this man's army instead of God's.

Cleaning the school concluded in time for the 6:00 a.m. prayer service and my first assignment of joining a street-preaching team under the leadership of a "lady general" from Germany. Unlike the softer Christine back in Bozeman, this German sister was living proof of what the *Principle* says about God's all-powerful nature being every bit as evident in woman as in man.

At twenty-three I hadn't yet formed any real criteria for classifying what constituted a crazy person; but preaching to strangers on a street corner would have been high on my list. Armored for the day's battle with songs and prayer, we told passersby's in front of the Empire State Building about God's coming hope for America. Terrified of just about everything in New York, I was most afraid of speaking in public—especially to an audience so much in a hurry they didn't give a damn. Instead of stockbrokers and bankers, 34th Street's homeless and resident derelicts made up the bulk of our motley congregation.

Returning that evening from bringing down judgment on the modern day equivalent of Sodom and Gomorrah, I climbed the Center's marble steps and abruptly threw up. A combination of culture shock, the realization of suddenly having become a religious zealot and the smell of urine in front of Penn Station all contributed to the vomiting of my stomach contents on that first day in the Big Apple. Contemplating a call back to the members in Missoula to see if I'd actually come to the right religious group, I fell asleep praying about the answer I knew to be true.

By 1972 the American Movement had sold enough scented candles and secured enough personal loans from members to purchase the Belvedere Estate in Tarrytown. Next to legendary Sleepy Hollow and the Lyndhurst historic mansion of Robber Baron Jay Gould, Belvedere became the first American home of Reverend Moon and the place at 5:00 a.m. every Sunday morning members came to hear him speak. A far cry from the tiny shack he built with discarded American munitions boxes in the refugee camps of Pusan in 1954, the estate and its 35 acres overlooking the Hudson River was such a serene setting to see him for the very first time.

For some forgotten reason, the New York members took me to Belvedere on a midweek visit. Approaching the holy ground where the Reverend frequently prayed, I saw him off in the distance standing on his prayer rock overlooking the Hudson. Unaware I was watching, he stood quietly with both arms crossed and hip cocked. Gazing wistfully beyond the bank before him, it seemed his thoughts were carrying him elsewhere…like the river at his feet.

With Reverend Moon and fellow Chico Wildcat, Mike Leone, 1976

Before meeting Reverend Moon, I'd heard how Jesus appeared to him while deep in prayer at the age of sixteen on an Easter Sunday in 1936– asking the young Korean to complete his mission. I'd been told the tales of his endless tears and many tortures. I knew all the things a believer would learn, making him seem larger than life. I'd viewed him from afar through the biographical binoculars the Church had provided. Now I'd have the chance to see him through the microscope of my own experience.

37

Meeting Reverend Moon

SEEING AND HEARING REVEREND MOON is one thing. Knowing him is another. Even though he's the figure who re-introduced me to God, arranged an unusually happy marriage and has managed to get me to think about him at least once a day for the past thirty-four years, I cannot say I understand him. But there was a time when I was around him quite a bit.

Like when he was preaching an early morning sermon at an upper west side Manhattan church before the Yankee Stadium rally. Inspired as usual, he went beyond the time allotted by the Protestant church we were using. Outside, the elderly congregation gathered at their usual hour. And they were no doubt puzzled seeing the hundreds of young faces seated in their regular places in the pews. Their sharp-featured pastor came out on the pulpit and angrily pointed at his watch to Reverend Moon's interpreter, who knew better than to interrupt him in the middle of a message. The minister then did the next best thing he could think of. He climbed up the balcony and began playing the cathedral's giant pipe organ. "Once to Every Man and Nation" got his point across and the Reverend concluded his talk.

Reverend Moon then led a procession of adoring members out through the vestibule of the church. The minister continued playing the organ, accompanied by a stare guaranteed to send sinners, and especially my Korean savior, straight to Hell. Standing in-between the two men, I watched for Reverend Moon's reaction. He looked up at old Pastor "Long Shanks" (or whatever his name was) straight in the eye and smiled, exuding all matter of warmth at his theological adversary. A smile snuck up on his face and before long the minister stopped playing the organ. It's been said that love conquers all. Fifty-eight years on earth have taught me it's not that simple. In that moment, the Reverend demonstrated that kindness is the best method to use when trying to build bridges between faiths.

One of my proudest moments was on a night he said nothing at all. It was at the U.N.'s Grand Assembly Hall in December 1973 and he'd presented the Korean children's dance troupe, the Little Angels, for the benefit of the United Nations Children's Fund (UNICEF). I'd been part of a public-relations team that invited New York's blue bloods from Wall Street and Park Avenue to attend the first-ever cultural performance at the hall the world's diplomats normally use to utter their double-speak. His large family had just come from Korea and the young ones adorned the aisles around him. The Reverend was introduced to the gathering from a regular seat in the audience. A heartfelt applause followed the acknowledgement and preceded the only nice things I ever recall *The New York Times* writing about him. I was proud not only of his recognition but of the good we had done. Unfortunately, once Reverend Moon began teaching his revelation to the religious Establishment is when he got himself into trouble.

In advance of his speech at Madison Square Garden on September

18, 1974, I was assigned to the Columbia University area in Uptown Manhattan. Upper West Side New York liberals, many of them Jewish, were not all that interested in hearing what a Korean Christian prophet had to tell them. We found more receptive listeners in nearby Spanish Harlem than we did around Columbia's Hamilton Hall.

The smell of coriander and plantains frying inside doorways with the occasional East Indian curries comprised a tantalizing sensation while wandering New York tenement hallways. Prospecting there for guests was less tempting than the Columbia dorms, where the smell of marijuana, incense and beer were a reminder of a chapter in life I'd already closed.

The Movement created quite a stir with its throngs of finely scrubbed members descending on the bustling streets of New York's five boroughs. Enough posters inviting the public to come to a "Re-birthday on September 18th" were plastered on subway walls, burned-out storefronts and Manhattan buses, to make most New Yorkers think Sun Myung Moon was running for mayor.

The night before the spiritual showdown happened at the Garden, the Church hosted a gala banquet at the nearby Waldorf Astoria. It was such a big deal my mother flew in for the occasion. The main banquet hall was filled to capacity and Reverend Moon was at his charming best. The Church even got Jeanne Dixon to sit at the head table. While introducing Reverend Moon, the crowd and no doubt the Movement's organizers who paid her hefty honorarium, waited anxiously for her to "reveal" as other psychics like Arthur Ford had, about the mission of our new messiah. After a litany of boring self-promotions, she finally delivered a series of theologically safe platitudes on behalf of the evening's host.

Reverend Moon took the stage to guarded applause from 3,000 of New York's curious elite in attendance that night at the Waldorf. He began by apologizing for all the inconveniences members caused New Yorkers during their daily commutes. He humored the audience with poignant examples about the value of living for the sake of others. At one point he spoke of a young couple he'd witnessed with a newborn, he said, "looked like an Idaho potato," proving how God-like and blind a parent's love of children is.

A demonstrator from the People's Revolutionary Party jumped up on the table next to where my mother and I were seated and entertained those in the ballroom before being dragged away. All in all, it was an exciting evening. The audience wasn't aware that what Reverend Moon was serving up were mere spiritual hors d'oeuvres compared to the full course of his religiosity that would come the following night at Madison Square Garden.

The next evening, thousands were turned away, including the busload of East Indians and Puerto Ricans I'd brought down to lower Manhattan from 123rd Street. Ecstatic to see the overflow crowd, I abandoned my guests to a disappointing return trip to East Harlem. Pretending to be a church official, I finagled my way through the masses and got myself inside.

Entering the Garden, I saw Reverend Moon singing a Korean folk song from the huge podium. He did so to quiet the fervent Communist and Christian activists who believed it was their Marxist and Evangelical mission to drown out his message. The singing worked. The crowd's sympathy, combined with the ushers' firm hands, removed most of the rabble-rousers. I was so excited by the size of the crowd, and the magnificence of Reverend Moon delivering his message on the stage of the modern day Rome, that I almost forgot my mom.

Searching the circular arena for my silver-haired mother was like looking for *Where's Waldo* in a United Nations haystack. Finally, about two-thirds of the way through the speech I saw her seated in an upper row looking haggard. The Japanese sister assigned to keep her company spoke little English and didn't know who in the world "Patrick-san" was anyway. I expected my mother to be inspired with all that Reverend Moon was telling the huge gathering about the Last Days, the Second Coming and the role America was playing at that critical moment in history. Instead, she was sitting there worried that her son had all but abandoned her on such a puzzling night in Midtown Manhattan.

My childhood friend Greg Keller also came to visit while I was in New York. Fresh off a divorce from the first wife who ran away with his brother-in-law, he traveled across the country to see me. I persuaded him to go to Barrytown, the former Christian Brothers Catholic Seminary the Movement purchased to hold its infamous weekend workshops. The problem was I didn't bother to attend with him. Not realizing he'd come to be comforted by his best friend, I instead presumed he'd been led by Providence to discover that Christ had come back to the earth. Greg didn't see it that way and left Barrytown to pitch his tent along the wooded shore of the Hudson River in a physical environment he felt more comfortable in than the religion-charged one I'd invited him to.

At that point in my life, I was a good disciple but a horrible friend. Years later I overheard a pastor in Watts say about the very religious, "Some are so heavenly bound, they're no earthly good!" That applied to me in my early days in the Movement. In those times, I'd passionately put the needs of "Heaven" ahead of my guests, my mother and my childhood best buddy—all of whom were residing squarely here on earth. I seemingly was living on some distant plain.

38

Sunny Side of the Moon

ONE MORNING I KNEELED BESIDE my cleaning companion, Wesley Samuels. The first black member in America, Mr. Samuels is a dignified gentleman with the kind of soft facial features only someone with an African heritage can have. I couldn't help but overhear his prayer. Asking God for the forgiveness of bygone slave owners, his tearful plea pierced to the heart of my white American soul. His tender mercies brought me to a full-blown repentance for every sin I or my ancestors had ever committed—and then some. Normally, reconciliation requires someone saying they're sorry before the other can say I forgive. Wesley, like Jesus, put the cart before the horse, helping me to feel forgiven without doing anything to deserve it.

Millions of Wesley Samuelses—like their dark-skinned predecessor, Simon from Cyrene—have borne the white man's burden carrying Christ's cross. It's a good thing for America that African slaves and their descendants found Christianity with its propensity to forgive before discovering Islam and its penchant for justice.

Another race and nationality where historical restoration was required of me were the Japanese. In spite of the foxhole pact my father made with a handful of Nippon soldiers in Burma, his generation's animosities persisted and some element of them were no doubt deposited in my genes.

The challenge of loving, and even marrying one's historical enemy, is an important element of Unification beliefs. Providing American members with the opportunity to restore relations with a recent foe, Reverend Moon brought thousands of Japanese with him to the United States in the early 1970s. The descendants of Bible-touting Western Europeans were now getting the reverse conversion treatment by evangelizers from the Far East laboring in the American mission field of the late 20th Century.

Prominent among them was a Japanese Church leader by the name of Takeru Kamiyama. A towering spiritual figure in the lives of the members who worked under him, he was charged with raising the finances for the American Movement. He also saw it as his mission to break the shackles of individualism he perceived had a hold of most Americans. Kamiyama's blend of Eastern wisdom and spiritual bravado captivated Western members in the same way the Ken Watanabe character "Katsumoto" did Tom Cruise, in *The Last Samurai*. Taecho (or boss), as he was affectionately addressed by his inner circle, once said when the Kingdom was built, he'd take a bath in beer! That statement alone was almost enough to dissolve any historical resentment I'd harbored against him or his countrymen.

The son of a rare Christian clergyman in Japan, he explained in a moment of late-night candor why he thought Christianity had never gained a foothold in Japan. Kamiyama-san said that when the Japanese were presented with the Gospel, they perceived Jesus to be less than a perfect Master. Given that his disciples were disloyal and deserted him in his darkest hour on the cross, traditional Japanese thought there must have been something lacking in his leadership.

Loyalty and fidelity were strange concepts to most young Americans. Mr. Kamiyama and the Japanese members adhered to those traditional Eastern values above all else. Even though it meant falling on a legal sword, Kamiyama went willingly to prison with Reverend Moon on what many civil-rights leaders thought were trumped-up tax-evasion charges. Remaining fiercely loyal to his leader, Mr. Kamiyama was the kind of disciple he believed Jesus should have had. Publicly shamed as only an Asian can be, Kamiyama wore black under his prison garb every day he spent with Reverend Moon cleaning latrines as guests of the American penal system in Danbury, Connecticut.

39

The Yellow Peril
Was Now Religious

PERCEPTIONS BEING WHAT THEY ARE in the Marshall McLuhan age of media, images of thousands of impressionable Americans sitting at the feet of an Oriental sage were easily construed to make Reverend Moon look like some authoritarian leader bent on self-aggrandizement. In a period when the young in America were leaving traditional churches and synagogues in droves, Reverend Moon appeared on the scene and was viewed by the media as a pied piper leading his legions of followers over the precipice of the Pacific Rim. Opponents, and even the well-meaning, were quick to label him the cause and not the effect of the problems mainline denominations were having in maintaining their flocks. The Yellow Peril was now religious, and the secular press was a willing accomplice in ballyhooing an image of a sinister Asian capturing the lost souls of America's sons and daughters.

Thus the term *Moonie* stuck. Sounding otherworldly, with an implied dark background, the label conjured up a picture of a mass following of a mysterious messianic figure—which in many ways was true. Reverend Moon once asked rhetorically why his American detractors never called the members Sunnies? Remembering my teammate Marty's antics in the back of the baseball bus, the answer was embarrassingly obvious--but never offered up. Members knew it was a pejorative term and mostly they were offended by it. But like the minority mindset that's incorporated the "N-word" into the African-American sub-culture, members eventually accepted the label and frequently refer to each other using the "M-word."

One night in a movie theater in the Bronx watching the Spielberg flick *Close Encounters of a Third Kind,* the moment in the film came when the aliens descended from the mother ship in full view of the terrified humans who stood in awe. As soon as the aliens appeared, a little girl seated in front of us turned and asked her mother, "Are they the Moonies?" I was tempted to tap her on the shoulder and say, "No, we are!" She would have screamed, so I left her alone with her misperceptions. The bunch of us looked at each other and laughed, not fully realizing that a public stigma had been attached to an identity that might take decades to remove.

Being misunderstood by the outside world was one thing. Judging one another on the inside could be just as destructive. After rising to the rank of a state director, I attended a leader's conference in Tarrytown with the founder. Seated with my fellow religious enthusiasts, a portly older gentleman caught my attention. He looked disheveled, a bit uncouth and frankly not the kind of leader I thought the Reverend deserved. Given my thoughts, a lesson I hope to never forget was about to be delivered.

As if to prove Jesus' point about finding the log in your own eye first, Reverend Moon did something unusual. He stopped the talk he was giving and had the man I'd been viewing with disdain stand up. He told how Peter Koch had once fasted for forty days in pioneering the path of the Church in his native Austria. Sitting there with two hundred others, the Reverend's antenna must have picked up on my negative channel. I was sorry and also amazed. Lesson learned; self-judgment is better than self-righteousness–especially if you want to avoid getting picked up by Heaven's radar speeding down the road to hell.

Despite finding a teaching that answered so many of my questions, new ones always arise before the answers catch up. Faith covers a multitude of doubts; but not them all. If Plato was right and beauty is in the eye of the beholder, is truth then in the mind of the believer? Believers believe so, but how much do we really know?

To this day, I marvel at the way the faithful view their religious leaders. Millions of Christians who never met him believe they have a "personal relationship" with Jesus Christ. How much of the real Jesus do they really know? Do they see him today as he truly was, or the way St. Paul and the Council of Nicea wanted him to be seen? Maybe the way most of us view God and those special figures in history who've helped people understand "Him," is through the prism of our own longing—getting back what images we need for our own edification. Even now, the way Japanese members view Reverend Moon is different than the way Americans do. Will he be seen differently by later generations of Unificationists and history? I'm sure he will. But I couldn't tell you how.

40

Life in the Lord's Trenches

THINKING I WAS PROGRESSING nicely in removing my "fallen nature" through a rigorous life of restoring things within myself and my collective past, I was happy the evening I came back to the Center from a day of doing the Lord's work. Pleased with my new-found spirituality, I was high on God's grace when I saw my two-hundred-dollar Bogner ski parka walk by on the back of another member. Wanting to say, "That's my jacket you're wearing," I caught myself from committing the worst of all sins in a communal environment, that of being self-centered. Living from a common closet wasn't such a bad thing, especially if you were trying to reverse a tendency of being a fancy lad–having been voted best-dressed for the class of 1968 at South Tahoe High. Hoping instead to lead a Gospel life of being clothed like the lilies of the field, it was better to dispose of fabrics made by Bogner and Brooks Brothers in the ash heap of my personal history.

With regard to restoration with a sworn enemy, I got my chance with Richard Nixon. In spite of the flash of forgiveness I felt at the time I joined for the man that represented, to many of us from the '60's, all that was wrong with America, I hadn't thought much about Nixon or politics since joining the Unification Church. Reverend Moon's decision to launch a campaign to "Forgive, Love and Unite" with the embattled Watergate figure gave me a chance to practice what he preached. Fearing the U.S. would make the same mistake in Vietnam that it made in abandoning North Korea to the Communists, he believed America would have stayed the course in Southeast Asia had not the Watergate scandal mortally wounded the presidency. The opportunity to fast and pray three days for Nixon on the steps of the U.S. Capitol was a lot not to swallow for a former draft resister. I justified it by thinking that if God could forgive me—the least I could do was to get over my hang-ups with the first ever, "I'm not a crook" president.

Mass rallies at Yankee Stadium and the Washington Monument were held by the Movement in the Bicentennial year of 1976. I headed up a large team of members in the Bronx preparing for the rally to be held in the house "that Ruth built." In advance of the program, we donned white jump suits and cleaned the grimy streets around the Stadium to symbolize what we believed the Movement was spiritually doing for America. Residents around Fordham Avenue, whose streets were never swept like the City routinely did for the merchants of Manhattan, resented the implication their neighborhood was dirty. We nonetheless showed up every day to gather their garbage and in effect judge them, for not keeping their own front yards clean.

New York City opinion leaders barely noticed our cleanliness-is-next-to Godliness campaign; but the Puerto Rican street gangs did. One evening, while going over the day's results with my campaign team in our 157th Street storefront, a group of local hooligans tossed a smoke bomb in our midst and pulled down the roll-up door, leaving the lay missionaries to pray for deliverance. Undeterred by threats from the turf warriors or negativity in the press, we continued to scour the streets and search the tenements for guests until the Day of Judgment came on June 1st at Yankee Stadium.

Huge gusts of wind from a freak thunderstorm and hordes of Christian and Communist protestors failed to spoil the "God Bless America Festival." The members nervously sang, "You Are My Sunshine," until the rain stopped. The crowds filtered in and Reverend Moon delivered his speech. Later that night, Mr. Kamiyama led a group of us in a Jericho-like march seven times around the Stadium, singing holy songs and making our offering to the high heavens. The poor Yankees security personnel had never seen such a strange group of revelers, except for the time 28 years later when the Red Sox beat the pin strippers in the sixth game of the 2004 American League final.

If New York City is the equivalent of Sodom and Gomorrah, then Washington D.C. was the reincarnation of ancient Rome. Believing if Jesus had been triumphant in Israel, he would have traveled to the Roman Coliseum to deliver his message to the world, Reverend Moon intended to do no less in America's capital. Just three months after the rally at Yankee Stadium, the Church staged another huge event at the Washington Monument on September 18, 1976. The Church's P.R. person, Michael Smith, teamed up with legendary ad man Stephen Baker of "Let your fingers do the walking" fame, and came up with the slogan: "Meet us at the Monument!" Being the Bicentennial year, patriotic celebrations were in order. A gigantic fireworks display and festival atmosphere insured that hundreds of thousands of onlookers would turn out to hear "America and God's Will" from the Reverend.

I saw my first bear near the cabin today. The size of it scared me. It wasn't as big as the one my son Daemin and Tom McDevitt's son Joe claimed to have seen coming back that day from chopping wood on the land. To hear their account, the two of them witnessed a gigantic descendant of the last Grizzly seen in California in 1903. My bear wasn't anything like their exaggerated sighting. To put it more dangerously, it was just a cub.

I'd just landed my second Rainbow of the day on the wild sloping section of the Little Walker River below Willow Flats. My fishing companion and Dingo-looking pound puppy, Sunny, tore after the Black Bear youngster just as I was taking the hook out of the mouth of my catch. What worried me was, I'd already violated the first rule of fishing in bear country, that of failing to bring along a friend who was a slower runner than me. By myself, I couldn't help wondering if I was in the unenviable position of being between the cub and its worried parent. Showing no fear and a dog-sized brain, Sunny chased the cub back in the direction of its mother. I didn't bother following to investigate, but since the sow didn't show up and slap me silly for threatening her offspring, Sunny and I both quickly returned to the cabin unscathed—but looking back warily over our shoulders every step of the way.

Irate bears were one thing to fear later in life; but running into satisfied suburban housewives from Chevy Chase bent on protecting their young from the clutches of Reverend Moon could be just as frightening. The District of Columbia was divided into twelve districts for the Washington Monument campaign. The tribe I was leading was responsible for the suburb where every home was a perfect picture of upper-middle-class contentment. From outward appearances, they were in no need of salvation from me or my Korean savior. Roberta Flack's "Killing Me Softly" was a popular song at the time and it felt like it was written with me in mind. Whenever my invitation was rejected by a housewife oozing with condescending politeness, it was guaranteed to suck the life out of a wide-eyed optimist like myself.

The 11 other tribes had areas in the District with considerably more black family households than Chevy Chase. African-Americans were generally kinder to our members and more receptive to a message honoring God's role in the founding of America. Twentieth Century smug white housewives didn't need to be reminded by strangers that God should be thanked in the year 1976. Consequently, my tribe's results in terms of confirmed guests to the festival were far lower than my fellow leaders. Growing within me was an increasing sense that I might be the "Judas" of the twelve tribal disciples–failing Christ at his appointed hour. I wondered if I, like Judas, had somehow sinned by misusing public money or secretly doubting the veracity of the Reverend's messianic claims.

Weary of praying and repenting for the lack of "sure-sure" guests to report to Neil Salonen, I took my trusted assistant Bruce Boninni with me late one night to the holy ground. Thinking I might actually be possessed by the spirit of the betrayer, I asked Bruce to deliver a haymaker to my chops in hopes of jarring loose the evil one; or at least knock some sense into my head. Puzzled by the request, he reluctantly complied. The self-imposed "exorcism" didn't work. All I ended up with was a sore jaw and a confused assistant. The campaign concluded with the anticipated meager results from Chevy Chase; in spite of the dark night of the soul boxing with my demons and Boninni at the prayer tree.

The fateful day arrived and I boarded with what guests I could gather on a bus from Chevy Chase headed for the Ellipse. Overhearing an initial radio report telling of clogged streets and smaller-than-anticipated crowds, my mind conjured up scenarios full of fear and failure. Finally reaching the Monument, people were everywhere. Fearful tears turned to ecstasy. The crowd was immense. The Park Service estimated it at over 200,000. The Church later calculated

300,000; including the spirits of history's saints and sages we were confident were in attendance. Beaming ear-to-ear, Reverend Moon walked on the red, white and blue stage and called upon the "three brother nations of Israel, the United States and Korea to join hands in a unified effort," contributing "internally to the unification of world religions and externally to the unification of the world itself." America may not have heeded his message. But at least they heard it.

The following week I was selected to teach a workshop with hundreds of curious attendees from the Monument event, including a woman reporter from the *Washington Post*. She wasn't there to be converted but to give a description, among other important observations, of the type of suit I was wearing. Writing that I resembled a "J.C. Penney's mannequin," she wasn't far from the truth, since as a penniless missionary, I certainly wasn't buying my threads at Macy's anymore. She glossed over whatever profound truths were presented. Still, I didn't bother to take issue with her after the article was published. Figuring a secular newsperson from the Roman Post 2,000 years ago would have also missed what Jesus was saying–preferring to comment instead on Peter's fish-stained robe or Mary Magdalene's fishnet stockings.

41

Pioneering the Lone Star State

FOLLOWING THE FESTIVITIES in the nation's capital, I was sent to Texas to pioneer the Church. Assigned a handful of new members, we arrived and established a center in Houston. Knowing next to nothing about the neighborhood we moved into, I later discovered the Montrose District was home to both Houston's gay community and its largest concentration of nudie bars. Oh, the Hare Krishnas lived nearby as well.

After finding our first convert, a young woman architect from Taiwan by the name of Alice, I thought how to use her talents to make a splash for our fledgling efforts in the Lone Star State. Not having the membership base or finances to design and build an edifice worthy of the Movement's lofty ideals, I utilized Alice's artistic gifts to deal with the pornography presence in our midst. Besides having the drawing dexterity that all architects possess, Alice knew how to make a sticky paste out of boiled rice that was stronger than Super Glue, but washable. The two skills converged in creating beautiful paper-Mache

Victorian-style dresses that could be made to stick to the larger-than-life neon nudes that decorated Montrose's main street.

Hoping to craft a public-relations angle for the planned late-night "cover-up," I notified the media in advance, that as the person "responsible for dressing up Montrose's nudes," I'd turn myself in at noon the next day in front of Houston's City Hall. Not wanting to be charged with destroying property, I offered to "work side-by-side with the club owners to do an honest day's work in the sun," to remove Alice's frilly fashions. The Associated Press covered the spectacle and sent the news so far and wide it reached my puzzled parents by way of the *Tahoe Daily Tribune*. The bar managers got their kitchen staffs to remove the pasty garb from the nudes and the Montrose District returned to its normal unadulterated presentation of the feminine physique. The Church ended up getting enough local notoriety that the *Houston Chronicle* visited the Center and did a front-page story on how the Unification Church was threatening the very foundations of Western civilization. It occurred to me some time later that if they thought Reverend Moon was such a threat, they should have waited 25 years for Osama Bin Ladan to come along and report on someone literally destroying the foundations of Wall Street!

The other part of the Montrose district not directly visible, and even harder for me to decipher, was the gay community. At that time, the Movement was beginning an outreach program called "Home Church." The tactic employed was to select 360 homes in a neighborhood representing the 360 degrees of a globe, symbolizing the world. You were to visit, get to know to folks, perform community service projects and generally become close enough to the people you'd contacted to have them become interested in what you had to teach. The challenge facing me was that of the 360 homes in my representative world, about 150 of them had homosexual men residing together. As sweet as some of the guys were, most had other things on their mind beside hearing a message from me about God's ideal being a man and a woman joined together in eternal marriage.

If the more risqué parts of the Houston neighborhood we lived in were represented by a G-string, there were at least other parts of Texas more closely resembling a belt. *The Bible Belt, t*hat is. Or more precisely, the "buckle of the Bible belt," if you included Lubbock, which is reputed to have more churches per block than anywhere on earth except the Vatican.

Mike Jenkins was from the first graduating class of the Unification Theological Seminary and was sent to Austin to begin a ministry in Texas's premier party town. Mike's a loving and strong-willed fellow who since has rose to the rank of president of the Church in America. We became close friends and took turns teaching weekend workshops where a number of new members joined.

Looking to baptize our converts in the fire of a makeshift evangelical crusade, we set off on a tour of Texas that took us into the heart of the Biblical buckle in Lubbock. Holding a program near the campus of Lubbock Christian College, a Church of Christ-affiliated institution, we attracted an audience of clean-cut young believers who looked just like us.

It was Mike's turn to deliver the message. I was in charge of warming up the crowd with music and song. Jenkins had apparently fallen asleep during his seminary class on Christian Denominations in America. Not remembering that the Texas branch of the Church of Christ had splintered over an obscure passage in the Old Testament forbidding the playing of instruments during worship, we were in for a few awkward musical moments with our attentive audience. Accompanied by guitar, I started the program off with a Christian hymn I assumed everyone knew. Noticing only our members singing along, I wondered if my guitar playing was really as bad as had been rumored. Finally, a guest from the back row shouted, "Try it without the guitar!" I did, and the entire room joined in the chorus. Thinking they were now warmed up, I resumed strumming the chords on my twelve-string. Once again, silence from the Christian crowd. After the program and minus the music, both groups enjoyed a nervous laugh together. Neither side converted the other.

The Jenkins and Hickey crusade kept on rolling–running into one Lone Star character after another. Presenting my "Jesus didn't come to die" message in Lufkin, New Testament pages were flipping so fast and furious it felt like a Texas twister had squeezed into the rented hall. Following a grueling question-and-answer session, a Christian evangelist oozing with sincerity cornered me and told me in his right Texan twang, "I love you, Pat, but if you keep following that Moon— you're going straight to hell!" I thanked him for the warning but felt certain in that moment that if I was bound for a life in the lower depths, it was because I believed God and my friend Jenkins were leading me there.

We later rented an East Texas farmhouse between Lufkin and Nacogdoches and converted the barn into a lecture hall. Weekend workshops were held there and guests came from as far as Arkansas, Oklahoma and Louisiana to hear Jenkins and me teach the Principle on a large whiteboard under the hayloft.

The locals weren't paying much attention to all the shenanigans their Congressman Charlie Wilson was up to in Washington, but they did see us coming. A front page story in the *Lufkin Daily News* foretold of our arrival in Angelina County. An article on the "Moonies coming to town" appeared beneath a photo of stampeding elephants in New Delhi, which gave townspeople the impression we were about to run roughshod over them and everything that East Texas stood for. The result was a regular procession of pickup trucks on Friday night driving slowly by on the dirt road in front of the farm after the high school football game was over. The stream of vehicles looked like the scene from *Field of Dreams* when Iowans went out to see for themselves the crazy thing Kevin Costner had done in the middle of his cornfield.

We'd faithfully put in a call to the local sheriff. He'd show up and park his cruiser in front of the farmhouse and encourage the good ole boys (all of whom he knew on a first-name basis) to hurry along. One night a few of the braver ones attempted to burn a cross on our volleyball net, but that was the closest we came to be tarred and feathered and run out of East Texas. Probably it was because the locals were more afraid of us than we were of them. Nothing too serious ever happened except for the commotion caused when Houston Oilers quarterback Dan Pastorini showed up one afternoon trying to intimidate a Rice University student to go back to school and his parents in Utah. Jenkins, who'd wrestled and played football in high school, stood his ground against Pastorini—who seemingly didn't want to chance a tussle and add to an already injury-prone career on the gridiron.

The Rice student's parents had been pleased to get him out of Utah and the reach of the Mormons. Now being in Texas, he stumbled into the sphere of the "Moon" that was on the rise on college campuses. Knowing the Church was facing a public-relations problem from this wealthy family who'd doled out their cash to send their son to an elite institution, I tried to convince the young man to stay in Rice and finish his degree. John found life in the Center to be more satisfying than in the dorm with his slide-rule-toting engineering roommates; and he rejected my advice. Sensing the growing tensions we were creating in Texas, I organized a first-ever parents' conference. A number of supportive family members and the terrified parents of the young man from Salt Lake attended the informational meeting with Neil Salonen, the Church's president at the time. Advised by deprogrammers to play along in order not to tip their son off that something was in the works, his mom and dad came to the conference pretending to be respectful of the wishes of their adult-age son. At the same time they had put the wheels in motion to have him kidnapped and deprogrammed once the conference was over; which they did.

My own parents were approached by deprogrammers. It was quite a lucrative business during the 1970's. Families who'd been traumatized by media accounts of mind control and brainwashing by the various new religious movements were easily enticed into paying thousands of dollars to have the new faith of their offspring broken and even reversed. Having already encountered my hard-headedness in dropping out of school, refusing the Draft and generally marching to the beat of my own Aquarian-Age drummer, my parents passed on the opportunity to have me professionally "re-programmed" to their way of thinking. I'm grateful to this day for their temperance.

A year later and John's short-lived faith out the door, I visited the family's home in their upper-crust suburb outside of Salt Lake. His parents were polite but protective. Sensing their fear, I spared them the discomfort of having to deal with the issue and left wishing them well. I do hope John found his way in life—with or without the help the Mormons, the Muslims or whoever else may have attempted to provide him with answers to life's questions. If his parents had been wise, they would have allowed him the pain of charting his own right of passage into adulthood, like mine did. While my parents never understood or agreed with my choice, they never interfered with the path I chose. That fact, alone, helped heal our relationship as the years went by.

42

▼

Lonely Heart's Club Sect

NOW TWENTY-EIGHT AND HAVING taught countless workshops about a man and a woman finding marital bliss, loneliness began setting in. Drawing all those hypothetical "four-position foundation" circles on the blackboard about a family comprised of God, a husband, a wife and a child made me wish I actually had one.

Apparently my father knew something I didn't. He had a premonition about a marriage that I had no idea was in the works. Picking up the other end of the phone one night after the usual conversation with my mother about whether the Church was properly feeding and clothing me, my Dad got on the line and launched into an uncharacteristic tirade about the likelihood of me marrying "a rice eater." Appearing to either be having a flashback from his days in Burma or some unknown ancestral rage against the notion of interracial marriage, he hung up after warning me against bringing a child into this world from another race.

Taken aback by his unusual outburst and the fact that I had no plans for marriage at that point to an Oriental or any other sub-species, I frankly couldn't figure out what he was talking about. Ironically, what he said was about to come to pass; he just wasn't going to be the "father" arranging it.

Arranged marriages have long been performed by parents in traditional Eastern societies. Reverend and Mrs. Moon, who are seen as spiritual parents, began the custom in Unification circles in 1960 of arranging the marriages of their followers. Membership in the Movement was tantamount to preparing yourself for marriage with the faith that God was using the new Korean messiah to help find your marital match–presumably made in heaven.

Following our quiet little mass marriage affair at Madison Square Garden, Myung-Hee and I appeared together on the *Phil Donahue Show*. Phil asked pointedly, "Do you mean Reverend Moon said to you—here's this woman; she's the one for you and you're the one for her?" I answered, "More-or-less," but reminded him that many folks my age were routinely cruising single bars looking for the sequined light to go off on the disco floor over someone to seal the romantic deal with.

My marital odyssey began in October 1978 following a message that was left on the phone at the center in Houston. It said if I wanted to be considered for a "matching" to a Korean woman, I should FedEx an "8 x 10" color photo to the World Missions Department in New York by 4:00 p.m. the next day. This was one of the first times the Reverend had selected couples by picture and the also the first time he engaged a large group of Korean women with American men by applying his unique spiritual shake-and-bake formula to the art of matchmaking. Previously, he'd assembled the candidates in a room together, and made suggestions for their spouses. They then had the opportunity to at least look each other over, talk and pray about the selection before agreeing to it—or head for the hills if they didn't. In our case, a big-time leap of Kodak faith was being asked of both of us.

An older Japanese woman who'd been married in an earlier ceremony took me aside and had a "come to Jesus" meeting with me about what I was getting myself into. Mrs. Seino asked me to consider whether my family was prepared to accept an international marriage. Remembering my father's phone call, I said, "Apparently they were." She also pointed out that Korean women are unusually strong and independent for Asians, a fact Reverend Moon reiterated when I got around to thanking him for giving me a Korean wife, when he said, "You mean Korean knife!"

Although I'd not given much thought to what a union of "East" and "West" might produce, I remembered the beautiful son that John Lennon and Yoko Ono had brought into the world. Thinking that if I truly believed there was a "match made in Heaven" out there for me, this was the best way to give God a chance to demonstrate it. With this method, none of my worldly measurements played a role in selecting a mate. I left the matter in the hands of Providence (and the person in whom I had faith God was using) to locate my life partner. I went into the prayer room, offered one up, pulled the trigger and sent my picture off to New York. I felt at peace with my decision, even though I worried about what little the photographer had to work with. As it turned out, she was beautiful inside and out, making my act of blind faith not such a bad gamble after all.

43

My Moon Honey

I MET HER FOR THE FIRST TIME on top of a garbage heap in the sub-basement of the Boston Sheraton. It was the Thanksgiving holiday weekend of 1978 and Reverend Moon was hosting an international science conference at the hotel. The "picture matching" had just been completed in Seoul. The twenty or so men who'd been engaged to Korean women had only one thing on our minds–seeing a picture of our Moon honey! Colonel Pak, who was the Reverend's translator and chief assistant, had brought manila envelopes from Korea with photographs and introductory letters from our betrothed. In between his duties of attending the conference's host, the guys would ambush the Colonel on the way to his room, hoping to get the packet containing the visual particulars of their eternal female partner.

Wanting the moment to be just right, I waited until the final evening of the VIP event before making my move. Well after midnight, the weary translator came back to his room. Greeting him anxiously at the door, he told me he had barely a moment before returning to the Reverend's suite for a report on the day's activities. He whisked me into his room and pointed to a box on the dresser with the envelopes. I ruffled through it but, low and behold, no prize-winner for Pat! Preoccupied with his duties of attending the Reverend, Col. Pak assured me I had been matched and an envelope had been sent from Korea. He simply had no idea where it was.

But I did. What if it had fallen off the dresser in the shuffle and a careless maid had made the mistake of throwing it away? Having some experience with hotels from my days at Snowbird and garbage collection from my father's earlier enterprise, I knew that a facility as modern as the Sheraton probably had garbage shoots where maintenance supervisors dumped discarded waste. I went down to the front desk and explained my situation to the night manager who was already befuddled from all the conference organizers requests to smuggle Korean kimchi into the Reverend's suite. He summoned a security guard to escort me to the basement to oversee as I dug through mounds of yellow trash bags. Figuring I had nothing to loose and my eternal happiness to gain, I began my post-midnight pilgrimage through the Sheraton's garbage in search of true love.

After rummaging for two hours, I spotted the corner of an envelope protruding from a bag in the pile. Saying a prayer to be properly pure at the moment of my introduction, I opened the bag and found a manila folder with my name written on it, Korean style—"Hickey Patrick." Tears mingled with garbage stains and at exactly 2:58 a.m., on the morning of November 25, 1978, I saw her for the first time. I don't know what time it was at that hour in Korea, but I swear she was there with me in spirit—which is primarily how we would conduct our courtship for the next four years of our engagement.

Years later after we were together in Chicago, Reverend Moon visited the city and kidded me for being too close with my new spouse.

It was a problem for the Movement in its early days in America that had kept its young adherents zealous, in part, by keeping them chaste. Abstinence, I can assure you, does make the heart and other body parts grow fonder. Anyway, since he'd arranged my marriage in the first place, I told him he had no one to blame but himself. He laughed and I escaped judgment—at the least for the time being.

44

Romancing the Spirit

MYUNG-HEE WAS BORN NEAR the end of the Korean War as the fifth child in a family of six. Her grandparents were Confucian landowners whose home was on the southern tip of the Korean coast. Her father, like most Korean men of his generation, was forced to fight for the Japanese during World War II, where he was wounded in battle. Returning to his newly liberated country in 1945, it wasn't long before he donned another uniform against the invading North Korean Communists. During the war, the Presbyterians converted the Shin clan. For many Koreans, Christianity and democracy represented newfound hope and freedom after forty years of Japanese imperialism.

Her pious mother then had a dream that led her to follow a young minister from North Korea prophesying about the Second Coming. Many other spiritually inclined women in Korea were led in a similar fashion. They comprised the first congregation of early followers of Reverend Moon; who after being liberated from prison by Douglas MacArthur's U.N. forces landing at Inchon, had escaped to the South, where he set up preaching in the cardboard church he built above the refugee camps of Pusan.

Unlike many of the early female followers who, upon receiving revelations, never returned to their families, my wife's mother came home to her rural hamlet and led most of her Presbyterian relatives to follow the new teacher she'd seen in her dreams. Myung-Hee's father, by then a detective searching for North Koreans infiltrating the South, kept his favorite daughter close to him in police headquarters in Gwangju in order to attend better schools. Gifted academically, she had every intention of one day attending medical school. In spite of her father's suspicions, her mother's pre-dawn devotions and propensity to serve others led her to be part of the Unification Church from an early age. The Church was small and the settings were intimate in the early 1950's. On more than one occasion, Reverend Moon visited her family's home for a meal, with Myung-Hee and her siblings playing their childhood games around him.

As she prepared for her college entrance exams, the Reverend invited her along with a group of 120 students to study with him for one year at idyllic Chung-Pyung Lake, one hour north of Seoul. Thirty-three years later the Church erected a Vatican-like palace there for the royal members of the Moon clan. Then, it was a desolate Korean village with mud huts and grandiose visions around a campfire of the international community it would one day become. The prospect of enrolling in a "seminary without walls" was a huge test for the young woman who would one day become my spouse. Spending quality time with her spiritual teacher may have been a great honor, but it also meant giving up her dream of ever becoming a doctor.

In a meeting with the wary would-be seminarians, Reverend Moon singled her out as "someone with a big brain." Knowing she was struggling with his plan, the Church elders believed if she broke through, then others would follow. Her young Church friends watched carefully to see if she'd go along with the program or quietly slip away and attend university, which is every Korean's dream. Wrestling with the decision, she embarked on a twenty-one-day fast in hopes of receiving an answer. Even her devout mother thought the fast was over the top, but she persisted. Confined to bed for the final ten days of her condition, she had the experience of her spirit leaving the body. For the next few hours, she saw her life unfold before her like a full-length film. Included in the out-of-body journey was a glimpse of life at the lake and a mysterious Westerner who would be a part of her future.

Looking back, if Myung-Hee hadn't foregone those sixty-three meals and given up medical school, the two of us wouldn't be a pair. For that reason, I rarely turn down a chance to have a meal with my wife. Friday-evening dinners and a movie are something we now keep more religiously than church.

Scientists say it is brain chemicals in the bloodstream that makes a couple crazy when romance hits. Continents apart and never having met, surely something got into our neurons. Late nights in the Lufkin barn writing religious love letters and recording off-key renditions of John Denver songs to send along with them to Seoul cultivated all the romantic fable I needed. More than another's looks or touch, it's a state of mind that intoxicates a pair. We shared from our imaginations, which had more than a year to run wild before we ever met. Contributing to my dream state was the wistful picture she sent of herself in a grey sweater standing in the yellow grasses beneath Sorak Mountain.

45

Members Grew but the Movement Did Not

IN THE MEANTIME, I was appointed the Midwest Director of the Church in Chicago. The American Movement was going through a great transition in the early 1980's. Single members had joined by the thousands during the decade of the seventies and had dedicated themselves like only the celibate can. The era of single-minded devotion–behaving like priests and nuns–was about to change. Reverend Moon had begun matching thousands of couples in ceremonies in New York, Tokyo and Seoul, and new lifestyle changes were now being openly contemplated.

By then the Movement was full-scale into Home Church; which meant going door-to-door searching for new members and much-needed respect. Looking like Mormons, minus the white shirts and bicycles, members tried to blend into the communities they lived in. No easy task, given the image by then that most Americans had of the Church. The simple fact was we were not a part of their community. As Christ taught, we were "in the world, but not of it."

Reverend Moon taught that the two-parent family is life's primary "school of love." And while we idealized on blackboards about home and family, ours was a communal, not a nuclear family. When we spoke about church, most of those we talked with already had one of their own. Rarely stoned but frequently shunned, persecution in all its subtle forms was ever-present. Going door-to-door and leaving a doorstep to the sound of laughter inside nailed its own kind of cross to the heart. Persecution is good for the religious soul. Members grew. But the Movement did not.

The Church tried to be ecumenical, which is a smart strategy when you're an unpopular new religion. An opportunity to do so presented itself in October 1979 when Pope John Paul II visited Chicago. Believing the Polish Pontiff shared a kindred spirit with the Reverend because of their shared suffering at the hands of Communism, I directed the members to make a huge banner welcoming the Pope to the Windy City. A few dedicated members stayed up all night with our Catholic counterparts on Grant Park's grounds to guarantee the right spot to raise our show of support the following day. As it turned out, the banner was the only one its kind on display in the massive assembly. Such shows of affection had been banned by officials, but members' willingness to deprive themselves of sleep got the job done under the noses of the Catholic officials.

The next day we were front-and-center at the 1.5 million-person Mass on Lake Michigan's lakefront park. Seeing a photo of the banner on the UPI story that was picked up by newspapers worldwide, it seemed at the time a great victory had been won. Our sense of triumph, however, wasn't shared at the time by the throngs of adoring Catholics whose view of the Pope was blocked by our interfaith gesture. They tried, but didn't succeed, in burning us at the stakes that held the banner up.

The following night we stayed up again, this time outside Cardinal Cody's residence where the Pontiff slept for the evening. Perseverance was rewarded when the Pope appeared in the morning to give his papal blessing to the assembled crowd. According to the *Chicago Sun-Times*, the Pope "did a double-take when he saw a 30-foot banner that proclaimed in large red letters: 'We love the Pope, Unification Church'." Turning from the Moonies' display of interdenominational respect, the Pope made an up-up-and-away gesture, to the delight of the cheering spectators, and left the balcony."

Along with the sheer delight we felt for having gotten our message across, it was even a greater relief finally getting a decent night's sleep. As far as I know, nothing we did resulted in the Pope ever having an audience with Reverend Moon. His successor, Benedict XVI, then-Cardinal Ratzinger, was from 1981-2005 the Vatican's chief defender of Catholic orthodoxy and stood in the way of the Polish descendant of Peter ever meeting with our Korean patriarch. The fact that Reverend Moon would later arrange the marriage of African Archbishop Emmanuel Millingo didn't help matters. However, the Catholic hierarchy wasn't the only member of the Body of Christ bothered by the Unification Church's evangelism in the Windy City.

Following the assassination of Martin Luther King, Jesse Jackson had a falling out with Ralph Abernathy and the Southern Christian Leadership Conference. Reverend Jackson returned to Chicago, where he'd been a seminary student, and went on to establish Operation Push on the South Side of the city. His nephew Kenneth Gray had already finished a degree at New York University in engineering before completing two master's degrees in management and public policy at the University of Chicago. Jesse wisely had his eyes on his half-brother's son in hopes he'd one day become involved with PUSH.

That is until an unassuming young woman by the name of Kathy met Kenny outside his Near North Side flat. She invited Ken to a series of my lectures, and that was the last *People United to Serve Humanity* saw of his rising star.

As a Unificationist, Kenny went on to do the things he dreamed of and more. He traveled to Kenya as a foreign missionary to serve his beloved ancestry, became a Ph.D. and a Fulbright Scholar and was married by the Reverend to a white Rhodesian woman who gave him brightly colored and multi-talented daughters. One of them, Lacy, died in a car wreck in Morocco at the age of fifteen. Ken went looking for her in the spirit world a few years later, following death from a heart attack at 55 while doing what he loved– climbing a mountain in Tennessee.

I doubt Jesse Jackson ever forgave Reverend Moon for taking Kenny away. But as I see it, Kenneth Gray was someone both men could be proud of.

Sun Myung Moon once described his life as an encyclopedia of suffering. Imprisoned on six different occasions, he spoke frequently about life in a Communist concentration camp and how he found God in the midst of the most miserable of circumstances. In those days, I took seriously what he said and put myself in situations trying to connect with that "heart of God" he so frequently spoke of.

Like going alone pioneer witnessing for the Church for 40 days in Sault St. Marie, Michigan. I went without money or any place to stay. The first lesson learned was that the Great Lakes Upper Peninsula is one hell of a lot colder in August than Tahoe had been in March. Spending my first night near one of the Soo's famous locks, I found an old carpet in a dumpster and christened it a sleeping bag. Besides smelling like the cat that had previously inhabited it, the rug was nearly petrified, which made it impossible to roll up in.

The next day I persuaded a local flower-shop owner to donate a box of petunias to plant in a vacant lot beside City Hall. A young woman in the Mayor's office noticed my efforts and after talking she offered me a place to sleep on her couch. It was wonderful, until I realized the lonely girl had been reading too many of the Cosmopolitan magazines on her coffee table and was entertaining some ungodly thoughts about myself and the missionary position. I abruptly concluded my pioneering mission and went visiting my members throughout the Midwest who were having their own close encounters with the *Saturday Night Fever* culture of the early 1980's.

Another time I took a handful of members who'd all come from middle-class families and dropped them off alone for a day and a night in rural Illinois farming towns. Telling them to see what serendipity had in store, they had plenty to talk about when we got back together. In my town, I came across a crippled black man lying in a pile of bricks at the base of a Nineteenth Century building. Barely able to walk, his shiny skin looked like bright, chipped coal. His weary head was crowned with the most beautiful nappy white hair I'd ever seen. This African-American remnant of the prejudices of the previous century scratched out his living by cleaning the mortar off old bricks and selling them to a local builder for three cents a piece. I worked the day beside him in his pile. Beaten down by life's untold hardships, he barely uttered a word. But he understood my need for a place to stay. At the day's end, he brought me to his back-alley shack. It smelled of mildew and empty pork and beans cans. At that moment I stepped inside his place on the wrong side of the tracks, it felt like entering a living saint's temple.

The not long-for this-world gentleman's generosity trumped any act of kindness ever done for me. Dinner from a can tasted better than that banquet at the Waldorf. Falling asleep on his smelly couch, it reeked like my old friend the carpet in Sault St. Marie. Melancholy thoughts turned happy as I realized for the first time ever what Jesus meant when he taught, "Blessed are the poor…for theirs is the kingdom of heaven."

Should I be so lucky to meet Mr. Jefferson again, I pray he'll once again be kind enough to escort me along the streets of gold to the palace where he no doubt now resides.

46

Home Means Korea

FOURTEEN MONTHS OF DAYDREAMS and sleepless nights; I was on my way to meet Myung-Hee and her family in Korea.

It's difficult for someone from the West to understand what family means to a Korean. Like an Eastern saga of *The Waltons* and *Little House on the Prairie* rolled into one, their lives are bound together by centuries of history and family tradition. When Myung-Hee told me she'd had just three men in her life, she meant her father and two older brothers. Well, there were the numerous male Church admirers waiting in the wings who wished Reverend Moon's marriage plans for her had not included a foreigner. But to this pure Korean beauty, the only men that mattered to her before me were the male members of her own family.

The 16-hour flight to Seoul from Chicago stopped in Anchorage and caused me to reflect on just how far a little faith had brought me. The long journey jogged a memory of a boyhood dream of one day marrying an American Indian princess. Flying near Alaska's Aleutian

Islands, the plane crossed over the scattered landmass that many believe brought cousins of the Koreans to become our Native Americans. Maybe that was the connection in my dream. Maybe Myung-Hee, as her name means, was the "shinning princess" of my dream. Lucky for me, maybes were about finished.

The Korean Air flight was taking me to the Land of the Morning Calm. Meals and movies on the plane were all but ignored in lieu of re-looking at the pictures of the woman who would one day become the mother of my four children. Flipping through the photo album of my own Irish-American family, I realized ours was not merely a romantic union of religious lovers, but the melding of two family heritages about to be linked. We later met with an old Korean spiritualist in Seoul who said our two families were already celebrating in the next world. She wouldn't say if they were sipping ginseng or Guinness—but she assured us that partying was taking place.

Arriving in Seoul in early January, you're in for cold like you've never felt before. Americans who fought at Pork Chop Hill know of the dampening chill of the Korean Peninsula in dead of winter. Walking along the Capital's icy streets, the piercing humidity purges both body and soul. Fortunately, hot Korean food warms both.

It would be three days and two nights before meeting my betrothed. The Church would see to that. Three is a significant number in Unification circles. It represents the three sons of Adam, Jesus' three chief disciples and the three points of a circle symbolizing eternity; which is exactly what it felt like waiting to see her. My three days in the tomb were spent being lectured to by a Church professor on the providential significance of our marriage blessing. Besides giving a heavy dose of spiritual medicine deemed necessary to inoculate Americans from themselves, I sensed certain Korean male elders were bothered by the fact of Western men coming over to claim their fellow countrywomen the Reverend had given away in marriage. I listened dutifully to his talks, but my thoughts were plainly elsewhere. They were, by then, constantly with the 26-year-old black-haired woman who was on her way by train from the 38th Parallel hamlet where she'd been doing the Lord's work.

The first member of her family I met was her eldest brother. After the first day's talks, he took me to sleep in his home in a suburb of Seoul. To my shock, Myung-Hee's father was there in the house when I arrived! He sat Buddha-like on the floor, as is the Korean custom. Fortunately I came to my senses in time to fall forward in a full bow—which is customary in greeting a parent. He didn't smile or say anything; also typical for a Korean man. Had I been culturally only a Westerner, I'd have probably neglected to take off my shoes, strolled over and given him a good old boy handshake and said something unforgivable like, "nice to meet you, pops!" In my case, years of commiserating with Koreans and Japanese had sensitized me to the shallowness of most Western ways.

The moment to finally meet came during the third day of lectures at the Church Headquarters. By then, my mind resisted wrapping itself around any more of the pie-in-the-sky truths being presented. Dr. Sohn, my lecturer, also seemed tired of going through the paces of re-educating another American barbarian at the marital gate.

Giggles and nervous energy preceded her entry into the room. Escorted by a host of friends and relatives anxious to witness the moment we met, the office was abuzz with anticipation. Months of picturing her in my mind had created an image of a woman impossible to be as pretty as I'd dreamed. But she was. Shy but radiant, she came into my presence hiding behind her older brother. My first glimpse was of a hand reaching from around his back, grabbing for mine. It was more than love at first sight. It was a first touch that confirmed a love that had been felt but never seen.

After dinner with Church leaders and friends, we went to her brother's flat. Her father had returned to their country home, which we'd visit after our non-church Korean wedding. Before long, we'd be married a number of times, in a number of ways and in a number of places.

With Myung-Hee
Korea, 1980

Since all six of his children had participated in large Unification wedding ceremonies, the family thought the elder Shin deserved to have at least one chance to give away a daughter in marriage. Granted, it wasn't to be our true marriage. That would take place in three years along with two thousand other couples at a small gathering in Madison Square Garden. In fact, later when we thought of having a fourth wedding for the sake of my family in Lake Tahoe, I figured we were about to join Reverend Moon in the *Guinness Book of Records*. The Reverend's in there for marrying the most people at one time. I figured I'd get in for marrying the same person—the most times.

Given that sexual purity before marriage is the foremost virtue for any Unificationist, it was unbelievable to me that her family would have us sleeping in the same bed that first night we met. Compared to the puritanical undertones of Westernized Christianity, my Eastern in-laws believed the powers of faith and conscience were enough to warrant their trust. And so we dozed off into sweet slumber after pillow talk was concluded in the wee hours of our first night together.

The innocence of an occasional touch offered its healing balm and removed any emotional pain from my past. It seemed love could save a man. This religious relationship brought along with it the forgiveness that made a partial person whole again. My dreams were coming true and were embodied in the person lying beside me.

The rest of the three-week visit was a blur of wedding preparations, hiking Korea's magnificent peaks, visits to Buddhist temples, pilgrimages to the site of the Reverend's first church and walks along the Eastern Sea. The word vacation was not even in the vocabulary of a full-time member in those days—but if ever there was a time I felt completely carefree, it was during those 21 days in Korea. Those early times together were God's first installment in the promise of a family forever.

Meals consisted of all-Korean, all the time. Well, I did sneak away once from my crash course in cultural osmosis to the Commissary at the U.S. Army base in Seoul for a cheeseburger, fries and a chocolate shake. But for the most part, I relished being drawn into Korean culture through the Shin clan's numerous feasts. After dinners of barbecued kalbi, kimchi and rice, conversations carried on for hours. Eventually singing would be called for and the evening would come to a close. For someone raised by the constant companion of sitcom television, the simplicity of Korean family life was a truly human alternative. There in the South Korean countryside of her ancestral home, I found the welcoming glow of the large family I'd longed for as a boy.

It was hard to think of leaving her and surviving the separation period of three more years before our marriage would be "blessed" by

God. Thirty members of the extended family showed up at the airport for my return flight to the States. Lingering to the last minute before heading down the tarmac, I held back the tears that would have made me look childish, even though I felt like a newborn being torn from its mother's breast. In the span of three weeks, any pain from my past had all been erased. If deliverance from a life of incompleteness is one of the things a messiah does for you, then I met my savior in Seoul, and she would one day be my wife.

47

The Wilderness Period

MOSES WAS PROMISED CANAAN, but spent what seemed like forever in the desert before ever getting a glimpse. Like an Old Testament spy sent out by the Jewish patriarch, I'd viewed the Promised Land—but I'd have to wait to taste its milk with my honey. The separation course in my Midwest desert lasted three mysterious years laboring in the vineyard of my faith.

There, I saw my first Cubs game at Wrigley Field. I was introduced to Chicago politics by the local Polish alderman who left his indelible sign of patronage in the form of his name on the metal garbage can he delivered in the alley behind the Church. The politics of fear brought me down to the State Capitol in Springfield to fight the attempts of deprogrammers and the anti-cult crowd attempting to get the Illinois Legislature to impose a tax on all new religious movements. Twenty-five years later serving in the Nevada Legislature, the only ones vulnerable enough we could find to levy a new tax on were from a secular group of Vegas worshippers called tourists.

48

Down the Aisle of the Garden

OUR WEDDING DAY CAME on July 1, 1982. We took our vows standing
in rows before Reverend and Mrs. Moon, the media and thousands
of curious onlookers in the place the New York Knickerbockers call
home. Sharing the occasion with two thousand other couples at least
makes it virtually impossible to forget your anniversary every year.
Our nuptial bordered on the cosmic or the comical, depending on
your perspective. Even New York's finest swooned as they sat perched
upon their police horses along 34ᵗʰ Street watching us parade into the
Garden. A wedding, even a mass one, can touch a bystander's heart.
New Yorker policemen were like walnuts. Their sweet inner contents
spilled out once their tough veneer was cracked by a smile.

After years of fasting, abstaining and generally leading a rigorous
religious life, we were finally walking down the marital aisle. Even
though it was alongside two thousand other couples dressed in identical
blue suits and matching white wedding gowns, it was a momentous
day. We stood together--marrying for God, for history and, yes, for
ourselves.

In Unification thinking, the public purpose is always more important than one's private desires. Even with something as personal as marriage, you could be asked to forgo your rehearsal, as I was, in order to ensure that buses with guests coming from Harlem all had their seats filled and their box-lunches loaded. Despite the irritation of having to mobilize guests to attend my own wedding, we joyously entered the circular seating of the Garden to take our unique place in religious history.

Watching the endless procession of couples in front of us, tears flooded my face. More than the delight of being with my beloved, I cried seeing all those whom I'd known and worked with together for years on the frontline of ushering in the Kingdom. I saw in their faces the vibrant hope we all had for a world made up of families marrying to fulfill our purpose of creation. I knew firsthand the sacrifices many had made. Interracial and inter-religious marriages were easier preached than practiced. Oblivious to the sensationalistic media attention of this most unusual event, Myung-Hee and I stood with thousands of others proudly proclaiming our love. We visualized our two ancestries in the ramparts of the next world, dabbing their eyes like we were ours–happy to be looking down upon the beauty of our youth being offered to God.

**With Myung-Hee
at Rev. Moon's home
1983**

If you're waiting for an account of the wedding night—you'll have to wait 40 days (and nights) like the two of us did. Mr. Kamiyama, the Japanese fundraising leader, made sure of that. He was my wife's central figure prior to our marriage, and though I pleaded my case passionately (maybe too passionately, if you get my drift) for her to join me in my public ministry in Chicago, he joked it would be "good for me" to wait a little longer. He probably figured I needed an additional period of purification. Or more likely, "Heaven" needed another period of her fundraising result. Whatever the case, I took it as one more test along the road to my restoration. Ten years had been a long time waiting. But those next forty days seemed like the 40 years the Israelites spent lost looking to enter the Promised Land.

Myung-Hee was among only a handful of Korean women marrying with American husbands who didn't avoid joining the mobile fundraising teams that traveled the 50 states. Because she went, she met Americans that live in places like Helena, Montana and Bend, Oregon. She encountered the kind of people she would one day meet in my parents. It helped her to see another side of America in those rural states—and not just the cosmopolitan mish-mash that is a New York, Chicago or Los Angeles.

49

A Path to a Place None of Us Had Ever Been Before

WHEN SHE FINALLY ARRIVED in the Windy City, the Church members were as happy to see her as I was. Hungry for the embrace of a mother figure to comfort them as they too began their families, they looked to us to pioneer a path to a place none of us had ever been before. It helped that she was a "wise woman," as the Reverend had once said about her. The members sensed they had a lot to learn from her. And so would I.

To become the "ideal family" I'd been sketching diagrams of on the blackboard of my lectures, we first had to begin our family life. As with most Unification ceremonies, it was complicated. Without revealing the details of our first intimacies, suffice it to say accompanying our union of love was a religious ceremony reversing the Fall of Adam and Eve during a three-day ceremony. As providential as our religious honeymoon was, it seemed only appropriate that it be held in the bedroom, converted to a prayer room, that the Moon' stayed in whenever visiting Chicago. And as sacred (and anticipated) as each night was, it didn't prevent a member from one night knocking on the door asking, "Mr. Hickey, I'm sorry to disturb you—but Hiroko is looking for the keys to the van to pick up the fundraising team." The new Adam and Eve could wait until the members were picked up from their late-night flower run.

Single membership had been easy for the Movement. With the advent of families and the new ingredients of children and the money needed to support them, it was a challenge the Church was hardly prepared for. Visiting a married couple from an earlier Blessing with four young children in Cincinnati, they told of the burden they bore as the Center members had to fundraise extra hours to pay for their kids' school expenses.

During those first weeks together, Myung-Hee and I visited all ten states of the Midwest region. Full of hope for the future, and fears for their finances, members shared their hearts, especially with my wife. In the cold nights that are North Dakota, even our members slept early. We did too. Our first son was conceived on such a chilly autumn evening in the upper Midwest. But he wouldn't be born in Chicago as I'd hoped.

Reverend Moon thought it best that leaders be rotated and sent to small rural states. And so I drove my extremely pregnant wife through the snows of December to Vermont in the $400 Chevy Station Wagon I purchased sight unseen from a steel worker in Racine. The Church had been dormant in the "Green Mountain State" but still owned a small house on Burlington's main street. A handful of Japanese members were assigned us while a tubby Myung-Hee and I occupied a bedroom in the attic. The stairs leading up there were so steep I had to push with my shoulder under her behind to get her up into the bedroom at the end of the day. A mattress on the floor and her weary leg resting on mine are what I remember of those months together in the attic.

Our newfound happiness together didn't last. Providence, in the form of the new Korean Regional Director in Chicago, requested that Myung-Hee return to Rogers Park to serve as his interpreter. He was a kindly old family friend, and she agreed. Serving the whole purpose would bring us blessings. That was what we believed; and so it was true for us at the time.

The months without her in Burlington were lonely but afforded me the chance for a final fling at the last vestiges of single freedom. I could be as wild as a lay missionary with an inflated sense of morality could be. I challenged the ultra-liberal University of Vermont, which had let every pot smoker in the world from Long Island to Fort Lauderdale into her hallowed halls, to allow me to give a public address on campus. They refused and I wrote a rip-roaring Op-Ed piece in the Burlington Free Press which attracted the support of a Mormon Professor on campus who offered to co-sponsor the program the Administration was opposing. The founder of his unpopular faith, Joseph Smith, had been born near by; so the good professor had more than an academic interest in seeing a First Amendment freedom preserved for the newest kid on the spiritual block.

Feeling victorious following a presentation to a raucous campus audience, I decided to take a ride on my remaining wild side. I borrowed a beat-up motorcycle and set off on a tour visiting church holy grounds around the Granite State. The local paper, which had now taken an interest in my exploits, printed a photo of me leaving town on my Honda 250. An old downhill-ski-racing helmet made me look like the "Moon man" they alleged me of being. Taking off from Burlington in early spring, I was so layered and bundled up I looked more like the Michelin Man than a New Age version of Easy Rider. Along the way, I stopped in every town and hamlet that had a newspaper and told my story. I rode by ski legends Stowe and Mad River Glen dreaming that I could resurrect the name of Reverend Moon if I could challenge their best to a ski race.

While my son was growing in the womb, I was having my last hurrah—doing what I wanted to do without realizing all that I'd one day have to learn to become a father to a new family. Indicative of my wanderlust was the day I encountered a snowstorm near Montpelier. One thing was for sure, a motorcycle and snow aren't compatible. Luckily, a passing-by Vermont apple farmer threw my miniature hog in his pickup and hauled us both over the mountain pass. Like faith, you go so far before something greater than yourself, gets you over the barrier in front of you.

Myung-Hee returned from Chicago carrying inside her a son who would one day be dunking basketballs and throwing a four-seam fastball in the upper eighties. Not wanting to be a burden to the members, we decided to pay ourselves for his entry into the world at the local natural birthing center. Working nights and weekends after the church work was done, we raised the money for our firstborn without having to rely upon the good graces of our parents or the Church.

In Confucianism, you are thought to be an adult only after you've become a parent. The miracle of childbirth was providing us the chance to become both. I'd already been a believer. But I first understood the act of creation when I saw my E.T.-looking son being placed in the arms of my wife. "It's a boy," was my reaction to the nine-pound dream-come-true staring me in the eye! Tears of joy accompanied long-distance collect telephone calls to both our families. The cycle of single life was now over. Another mysterious phase began in its place. We were now parents.

Forty days later, we were invited to visit Reverend and Mrs. Moon at their home in upstate New York. Mrs. Moon held our son and the Reverend said to me, "So you're a father now." In that moment,

I laughed thinking that for the first time I truly had something in common with him. Confucius was right. My adulthood did begin with parenthood. And both would be a challenge.

50

Right Back
Where I Started From

THE SECLUSION OF VERMONT didn't last for long. The leadership cards were re-shuffled and we found ourselves back in California. Myung-Hee opened a nursery for the Movement's second generation, who were appearing on the scene in far greater numbers than any new members. It occurred to me at the time, if the Movement couldn't catch the mainline denominations by gaining converts, we could maybe do it the way the Catholics and the Mormons have done—by having tons of children! God knows the good folks that had been behaving like priests and nuns all those years were up to the task!

Heading up the Church's efforts in the Western States provided me an opportunity to return home in 1984. I brought to Reno a group we dubbed a "mobile" crusade team. Given there were eight pregnant women in the van, they were anything but mobile. We stayed for three weeks in one of Reno's low-rent dives down on West 2nd Street. It was the sort of place you'd see the numskulls of *Reno 911* rousting meth-heads and poor white trash from on late-night cable. As usual, we stirred up the proverbial publicity pot. And while my parents were happy to see us, I'm sure they would have been more comfortable had I continued generating controversy somewhere other than in their own backyard.

Teaching Christian Ministers
Lake Tahoe, 1984

I met with then-Governor Richard Bryan, who'd been to one of Reverend Moon's earliest speeches in Las Vegas and knew members of my family in the Silver State. I defended the Church on local television programs and was written up in the press. We arranged for a program at the University of Nevada in Reno to give my now-infamous lecture on Jesus not coming to be crucified. He may not have, but I was about to be by Robin Joyce, editor of UNR's student daily, the Sagebrush. Robin is the son of Nevada's legendary lobbyist, Jim Joyce. Beside his political pedigree, Robin was a devout Evangelical Christian who took his faith every bit as seriously as his politics. The result was a scorched-Moon editorial on the heresies of the Reverend and the efficacy of the University pulling the plug on my campus appearance. Having been down that road before at universities across the country, I mounted the religious-freedom horse and lambasted the young editor in an op-ed piece. The result was as expected–a boisterous overflow crowd at the

Student Union event. I never met my theological adversary at the time. But I would years later, having long since forgotten the incident, when I asked Robin to be my campaign manager.

Another spirited attendee was Rob Owens. Rob had just begun a fellowship for University athletes that eventually propelled him to become one of Reno's leading ministers. A former Special Forces guy, Pastor Rob was as righteous as he was bold. Not afraid to have his members come and hear what Reverend Moon was teaching, Rob brought them armed with their Bibles for a good, old-fashioned theological fight. And argue we did during the question-and-answer session. New Testament quotes flew back and forth like laser shots in an episode of 24. But even when battling Rob, you could count on it being done with a sense of respect that accompanied his convictions. Rob later attended an American Leadership Conference in Washington. And while he liked the conference themes, he never compromised his belief in the traditional way Christ is viewed. Seeing him some twenty-five years later at a Christmas party for his daughter, he's still the kind of gentleman a good Christian should be. And while I doubt I'm one of the five persons he expects to meet in Heaven, Rob's one of the most stand-up guys I know here on earth.

Another thing we did was to hold an informational meeting for area pastors at Reno's old Riverside Hotel. Among the area clergy that came out of curiosity were a husband and wife who'd been members of my very secular Chico State Ski Team. Kelly and Christi were just as cute as a married couple as they were when they were young racers. The thing about coming home was meeting real people from my past who knew me when I was more real. With the good response we got in Reno, folks thought we'd start a church there. But the Movement was still in gypsy mode and, when I did come back to Reno some 10 years later, I was more interested in living my beliefs than preaching them to others.

This was also the period that Reverend Moon entered Danbury Prison for tax evasion. It naturally became a period of the Church's commitment to religious freedom. Ecumenical outreach was helped by the perception among many religious and civil rights leaders that Reverend Moon's imprisonment in Danbury Penitentiary was the result of good old-fashioned bigotry. Historically, religions' founders have all faced their share of opposition and resistance. Moses was exiled. Christ was crucified. And to his followers, the persecution Reverend Moon received was a confirmation that he was walking the path that saints before him had trod. The Reverend's imprisonment in America brought more sympathy from the religious community than any of the public-relations maneuvers the Movement did to promote itself. Mainline denominations filed amicus briefs. Harvard law professors defended him in court. Even old-time-religion fundamentalists got on the First Amendment bandwagon, remembering what German Pastor Niemoller said about the Nazis: "…Then they came for me, and by that time no one was left to speak up."

51

Long Been
a Bastion of Freedom

THE BLACK CHURCH has long been a bastion of freedom. Its pastors rarely shy away from a fight against injustice. Reverend Cecil Murray of Los Angeles's First A.M.E. (FAME) Church responded to Reverend Moon's imprisonment without hesitation and spoke before a large gathering of ministers and freedom advocates at the Bonaventure Hotel in downtown Los Angeles.

Out of gatherings like that, a California Committee for Religious Freedom was assembled, composed of an odd assortment of flaming liberals whose hearts bleed so much they hemorrhaged. There were high-minded conservatives who ordinarily wouldn't associate with anyone else; civil rights activists amused to see an Asian religious figure going through what they had; and enough Mormons and Scientologists thrown in to make our meetings look like a Twenty-First Century spiritual salad bar. Common ground was maintained as long as everyone stayed focused on the First Amendment. Along with fighting the good fight, the Committee members were happy to be dialoging with men and women of the cloth they'd never associated with before. Religious agendas and judgment of the heretical, of which we were normally at the forefront of a pastor's indignation, were checked at the door during the week—only to be resumed at the pulpit on Sundays.

While in federal prison in Danbury, the Reverend did one thing that endeared him to at least some of his critics. He purchased a fleet of 250 U-Haul-like trucks and donated them to social activists and food banks in needy communities across the country. It was his way of trying to forgive an enemy who put him in prison. The trucks came in handy in Los Angeles when, in the wake of the Rodney King incident, riots in the Southland opened a bloody gash between Koreans and Blacks. Chip Murray's FAME became the headquarters for relief efforts to the nearby ravished neighborhoods. Members of the Hollywood elite, like Candice Bergman, stood side-by-side with African and Korean Americans and a spattering on non-descript Moonies trying to heal the wounds the riots poured their violent salt into.

Thirteen months later Reverend Moon was released from prison. A gala banquet was held in Washington, D.C. to welcome his return. National figures, from Orrin Hatch to Jerry Falwell and Joseph Lowery, occupied the head table and said important things about the state of religious freedom in America. The important thing to the Movement was—Reverend Moon was out of jail.

The Church would soon drop religious freedom as its cause celebre. Members of the California Coalition were disheartened because our members had been the glue and the funding mechanism that held the all the Lutherans, Methodists and cranky conservatives together. For the first time I was disappointed in the Church. We immediately changed gears to the anti-communist work of CAUSA—which had been successful in Latin American countering Liberation Theology.

This didn't sit well with our liberal friends in the California Coalition who had stood by our embattled side while Reverend Moon was imprisoned. They felt abandoned and, without saying it to my face, they thought our efforts may have been disingenuous. In that part of my mind that resided beneath my faith, I found myself agreeing.

Attempting to build a bridge between our liberal allies and the conservative agenda the Church was now pursuing, I came up with an idea for a symposium on the issue of South Africa. Conservatives could rail on the evils of a possible Marxist takeover, while our liberal friends could preach on the crimes of apartheid. Chip Murray agreed to co-chair the event that we held at the University of Southern California. We brought in venerable civil rights leader Dr. Ralph Abernathy, who went from that association to become the National Co-Chairman of the Movement's American Freedom Coalition. Eldridge Cleaver, once a radical,

With Eldridge Cleaver, Myung Hee and Rev. Chip Murray
USC, 1986

then a staunch anti-communist, was another panelist who attracted a good deal of media attention because of his past and present notorious views. *Starsky and Hutch* actor David Soul, even showed up–proving that Hollywood stars have too much time and money on their hands and routinely look for causes to give their lives meaning.

The Los Angeles Times took Reverend Murray to task for being "duped" into co-sponsoring with the likes of us. Chip was his usual thoughtful and un-apologetic self and defended the issue in his opening remarks, citing the "cause of lasting freedom on the African Continent as being too important to ignore."

It wasn't the first time Cecil Murray would take heat for his association with controversial figures gracing the pulpit of First A.M.E. Chip Murray was the kind of pastor whose door always was open. Anyone who got past soft-hearted receptionist Gloria got an audience with the man, from the crack-cocaine addict looking for a last-chance handout and the redeeming grace of his words, to button-downed officials from Arco and Disney who donated millions to the social ministries they saw as the only viable outlet to rebuild L.A. in the wake of the riots. They all got their chance with Chip. And Chip got the chance to practice his beloved Gospel.

In the process of being around him, I became a sort of adopted white son. With enough prayer and persistence, I could get Reverend Murray to go along with most of my schemes. Chip called me the "velvet hammer" to my face; and probably "slick" to his staff.

One of the last events we did together was a "Youth at Risk" symposium and awards presentation. Over 120 Southern California youth groups and community organizations came to showcase their good works. The event was followed by an evening Gospel fest in the main sanctuary.

Reverend Moon, in the hopes of finding a John the Baptist who could "make straight the way for the Lord" in American Christianity, commissioned three Protestant (and very white) Evangelicals under the auspices of one of the Movement's alphabet-soup concoctions–United to Service America (U.S.A.) to go around and hold revivals in major American churches. First A.M.E., Southern California's preeminent black mega-church, certainly fit the bill for the desired venue. Following the daytime youth programs, the three Baptist preachers each spoke that evening—ostensibly to give Cecil Murray and deserving others a "Diamond Award" for their meritorious service to God and His inner-city children. One of the speakers, Dr. Ronald

Godwin, a Vice-President at that time of the *Washington Times,* and the same man who years earlier had sent me stacks of "anti-Moon" literature after I'd interviewed Jerry Falwell for *Newsworld,* made the mistake of patronizing the Senior Pastor by saying in so many words that "he'd been to Billy Graham's church—and Cecil Murray's was every bit as clean and well organized." Translation: "Reverend Murray—you're not white but you're practically good enough to be!" Some of our members in attendance, sensitive to the historicity of the black-white religious dynamic, slithered in their seats looking for the nearest exit.

Following the Moral Majority Leader's remarks, Chip took the podium and spoke calmly to the three Anglo-Saxon wise men, without ever turning to address them. His lesson on the history of the Black Church and Christ's great commission to love was for the most part lost on the Movement's latest installments for the title of the great white hope; but not on me. Afterwards, in Reverend Murray's office, I apologized for the tone of the remarks. Chip comforted me in a way Jesus might have.

Curious about the workings of the mind of Reverend Moon, he asked why the Movement needed the assistance of "those three Nordic giants?" He wondered why the Church didn't have me or one of the other Unification leaders speak. It was difficult to give him the answer I knew to be true. The Movement, which originated in the Third World, was always looking for someone representing the First World's seat of power–to give it the justification it needed to return back to Korea victoriously.

After my remorse-session with Chip, he pulled out of his desk a Bozeman's whistle from his days as an Air Force major and fighter pilot in the Korean War, helping to save the fatherland of Reverend Moon. Myung-Hee was with me. There wasn't much we could say.

A hug and a tear were exchanged before departing to care for our Protestant elders who had come to First A.M.E. to teach–but not to learn.

I think often of the kind of pastor that Cecil Murray was. With the election of Barack Obama as president, Americans of all stripes will have the chance to work on whatever issues they have with race. I had my chance for historical restoration through the kindness of one Cecil L. Murray. As a former draft resister, I didn't have an Army token to give Reverend Murray in return. But I did buy him the best hand-tooled black-leather brief case I could find on the occasion of his retirement from FAME and his new professorship, teaching ethics at USC.

Another figure that came out of the experience of putting on the apartheid conference was Muazzam Gill. Attending the symposium on the behest of Dr. Ben Armstrong the two of us became acquainted and a relationship has evolved from the professional to the personal over the past twenty-two years. Originally from Pakistan, Dr. Gill served as a media man for presidents Bhutto and Zia-ul-Haq. A rare Christian in a Moslem inner circle, he foresaw the rise of Islamic fundamentalism long before it entered America's radar screen. Immigrating to the United States to take a position with the National Religious Broadcasters, he married Nancy, a pretty Pepperdine University co-ed who now principals a Lutheran School in Anaheim Hills.

Having majored in English Literature in the United Kingdom, Gill is capable of weaving a poetic phrase on the drop of a hat. One of them, "I'm a brown man married to a white woman with two olive children," depicts an image we both share as fathers of multiracial families. Another of Muazzam's celebrated barbs is frequently lobbed at congregations of white Evangelicals "Contrary to your beliefs, Jesus is not blond and blue-eyed and does not live in Newport Beach,

California!" And while it's true a prophet may not be a prophet to his own, Muazzam knows how to lay the wood on Western Christians like old Ezekiel did the Jews.

The two of us have traveled the globe from Berlin to Tokyo and London to Seoul attending the Movement's fact-finding tours and media conferences. Muazzam returned the favor by bringing a group of us to South Africa in 1986. Johannesburg business interests paid for a first-class trip of African-American civil rights activists and American church leaders to see the realities of apartheid–from their point of view.

Unable to visit the still-imprisoned Nelson Mandela, we did meet with some of the white Afrikaner representatives of Parliament who were responsible for putting him there. Even Dr. Bob Grant, conservative founder of Christian Voice, couldn't stomach the Dutch South African's Biblical interpretations of the Old Testament justifying the separation of races, and walked out of the briefing. Only Reverend James Bevel, chief strategist for Martin Luther King's "March on Washington" (who has since passed away and had legal and moral problems of his own), stayed and dialogued with the Afrikaner separatist. After meeting the Oxford-educated King of the Zulus and his wife number three, we spent the rest of the visit traipsing everywhere in South Africa from five-star hotels in Johannesburg to the shanty towns of Soweto.

Another such educational opportunity, in 1987, was traveling with a San Diego-based Christian Emergency Relief Team (C.E.R.T.) delivering medical supplies to Miskito Indian refugees along the Honduran-Nicaragua border. The Miskitos are an indigenous people the Sandinistas had "liberated" from their traditional way of life in the process of creating a new Nicaragua. In response, many of the Indians joined the Contras, the anti-Marxist insurgency the Reagan

Administration was quietly supporting. Our CERT party left Honduras in small boats loaded with food and medical supplies. Heading south, hugging the Miskito Coast to the mouth of the Rio Coco River, the only sounds were the hum out the outboards chugging and the seasick barfing.

A problem happened when we reached the mouth of the Rio Coco. The river separates Honduras and Nicaragua. The outgoing river's tides collided with the incoming waves of the Atlantic, causing our boats to overturn in the surf. All alone, except for the four Sandinista fishing vessels watching us through binoculars as we struggled to avoid a descent into Davey Jones's locker. The soggy crew made it to a sand bar in the river, which was preferable to being plucked out of the waves by the Nicaraguans and the international incident that would have ensued.

Most of our supplies were washed out to sea. An ex-Marine medic in our midst chopped up a tiny poisonous green snake before we made camp for the night. It didn't matter. The larger serpent had already struck. The mischievous sea creature that had wrapped itself around our boats had made sure our supplies would never reach the Miskitos.

After a half-day hike to a refugee camp on the Honduran side, we showed up with so little it was almost as disheartening for us as it was for the Indians who waited for us with wide eyes and even larger expectations. We spent a few days in the village as the medics and nurses among us did what they could to treat the victims of malaria and their bullet wounds. The Sandinista Army had just conducted a raid over the border a few days before. It was eerie to see the blood stains from a wounded woman on the staircase of the hut I slept in those few nights spent with a near-primitive people.

The sounds of war were ever-present at night and seemed closer than they actually were. The day before we left, the dark-skinned

Miskito soldiers returned from a foray into Nicaragua to tell their stories and enjoy a little R & R in the form of a baseball game versus the gringos from the North. Most of the fighting men were mere boys. I could imagine any one of them playing Donkey Kong back in an arcade in Pasadena. In moments like that, it was painful to be an American. These people looked to us as those who would understand their plight and come to their aid. In fact, Washington was debating the prospect in that very hour. But for those in the desolate camp along the Rio Coco, all we could do was to give the few packages of fish hooks and aspirin that had been rescued from the boats, and leave them literally with the clothes off our back.

With Miskito Indian soldier
Honduras, 1987

Twenty years before, I'd returned to Tahoe from paradise in Hawaii with nothing to wear. Then it was the result of a young American's wanderlust in search of pleasure. At least this time, arriving back in California without clothes, it was with a pierced heart for the poor who will always be asking, "If we are our brother's keeper?"

52

Hollywood Knights and Tinsel Armor

NOT ALL THOSE WHO SUFFERED at the hands of communism died in the jungle. One such victim fled to Hollywood and won an Academy Award before being killed by an Asian street gang, which may have had connections to the Khmer Rouge. Hang S. Ngor was a real-life Cambodian physician who played *New York Times* reporter Sydney Schanberg's interpreter, Dith Pran, in *The Killing Fields,* the cinematic account of Pol Pot's murderous regime in Cambodia.

It was difficult to take a bite out of lunch when seated with a person who'd been through what he had. Years before in Washington, D.C., I'd met another Cambodian refugee whose tale of suffering and sense of abandonment had made me re-think my opposition to the Vietnam War.

Following my meeting with the exiled doctor-turned actor, I arranged for him to speak at Reverend Moon's annual science conference being held that year on Thanksgiving weekend in Los Angeles. Hang Ngor, like anyone who had been tortured and lost family, had a horrific story to tell that went on far too long for the liking of the event's organizers. Scientists had assembled from around the globe and were at the mercy of jet lag and a sumptuous meal, making them far more interested in communing with their pillow than being lectured to by an impassioned victim of communism.

Making the evening even longer, another of my VIP guests, a retired County Commissioner from Santa Barbara by the name of Reginald Kerry, insisted upon leading the audience in three cheers of hip, hip and hooray for Reverend and Mrs. Moon, followed by a rousing rendition of "God Bless America." The molecular physicists from Bangladesh drew blanks as old Reg wailed away.

Such was the eclectic type of gatherings the Reverend presided over. He was patient to a fault, but I heard from certain Korean elders what a "bad show" it had been. Maybe it was like that two thousand years before when lowly disciples kept bringing lepers and the blind to Jesus for healing. He rarely said no, but it must have been a burden to his handlers. Just as my eccentric guests were pain-in-the asses to God's representatives on that star-studded night in La-La land.

One Hollywood figure I ran into one night was an earthly parent with his own cross to bear. Or so it seemed the evening I met Jon Voight at the Bonaventure Hotel. Having dinner with Dr. Don Sills, a red-blooded Baptist minister who headed up the Coalition for Religious Freedom, I noticed the Academy Award-winning star of *Midnight Cowboy, Deliverance, The Champ* and *Coming Home* reading an old book in a quiet corner of the restaurant. Seeing him there conjured up a memory of the night I saw The Champ in Seoul, on one of my early outings with Myung-Hee. The gut-wrenching account of little blond-haired Ricky Schroder losing his prize-fighting father to divorce and death was such a tear-jerker that Koreans, who love ridiculously passionate flicks, actually brought pillow cases to the movie hall to cry into. Anxious to tell the story of his sobbing Asian fans, I sauntered over to the actor's table with more than a little trepidation. After all, it is pretty presumptuous of anyone to invade the private space of a public figure, especially one relishing his time alone.

To my surprise, Voight welcomed me to his table. Maybe he needed a break from the heavy material he was reading about "the miserable path the saints have trod." I discovered the actor was a bit of a mystic and seeker in his own right. The Hollywood elite don't seem pleased with his newfound 21st century conservatism, but back in the 1980's he was squarely in their camp. His interest in the painful travails of humanity may have been exacerbated by being the father of actress Angelina Jolie, who was a teenager at the time and had just moved in with a boyfriend during her self-described "black period" when she aspired to be an undertaker. If rumor of the two's continued estrangement is true, then Jon Voight has suffered as saints sometimes do. That heart of an anxious father, so evident that night in the actor's face, is something even God must surely go through.

Another God-like figure in Hollywood, at least to conservatives, was Ronald Reagan. I had the privilege of being seated at a head table with the President and Mrs. Reagan in 1990. The former president was speaking at a gala event sponsored by the International Medical Corps that was honoring filmmaker and Church member Lee Shapiro. Lee had made a film,

**With President and Nancy Reagan
Hollywood, 1990**

Nicaragua Was Our Home, about the plight of the Miskito Indians that Reagan praised.

And Shapiro was in the process of shooting a second film in Afghanistan when he and his assistant James Lindelof were machine-gunned down by a Soviet airship. The President was not yet showing signs of the Alzheimer's that would later close the chapter on the man we all knew. That night he was vintage Gipper, giving a moving tribute to our slain brother and the valiant sacrifices that he and volunteer physicians had made in Afghanistan.

I had two great fears going into that evening. One was that I would be seated next to Nancy Reagan. The second, since it was a dinner dance, was that I might be required to dance with her. Besides imagining the Secret Service tackling me for an attack on her toes, I was equally afraid of having to make small talk with a First Lady. You know, light table chatter like, "So, what have you been doing with your life, Mr. Hickey?" "Thank you for asking, Mrs. Reagan. I'm fine. I just got back from selling flowers for Reverend Moon on Sunset Boulevard!" Dead silence.

As it turned out, I did sit next to her; but she did all the talking. I was honored to hear, probably for the 10,000th time, how she came up with the now infamous "Just Say No" campaign. I won't bore you, as she did the head table guests with just how the phrase was coined to get kids off drugs. But I suppose she was just as bored being there with me.

The kind nobility of President Reagan made me wish for more of the same in the White House. And maybe if the Unification Church had produced more brave souls like Lee Shapiro, Reverend Moon might have received the pardon the Movement sought unsuccessfully to get through Nevadan Paul Laxalt from the 40th president.

53

Conservative Voice with a Korean Accent

FOR YEARS, CONSERVATIVES WERE FOND of saying that, if they had a nickel for every time someone said an alternative newspaper should be started up to counter the Washington Post, they'd have had the money to finance it! Well, no American ever stepped forward, but a Korean preacher did who put his nickels where their mouth was. Business interests related to the Reverend started the D.C. daily that finally addressed the problem of a one-party press in a two-party town. Ronald Reagan said it was the first paper he read every morning in the White House. Many Washingtonians applauded its content but pooh-poohed the founder. Nevertheless, the Movement gained credibility and clout under the umbrella of the *Washington Times.*

One conservative, who wasn't afraid to publicly acknowledge the founder, was Bruce Herschensohn. The Southern California journalist had a history with Reverend Moon. He'd been President Nixon's aide during the period Reverend Moon launched his "Forgive, Love and Unite" Campaign in support of the embattled Watergate president.

Bruce was there when Nixon invited the Reverend to the White House and stood as perplexed as everyone else in the room was when Reverend Moon took almost the entire appointment in the Oval Office to pray fervently in Korean.

Bruce later returned to Los Angeles, where he served as a conservative commentator alongside liberal John Tunney in KABC TV's legendary point-counter- point segment on the nightly news. Such civility between two rivals has not been seen since. The angry talking heads we see on today's cable networks pale in comparison to the enlightened exchanges between those two, who were both friends and foes.

Before his second try at a U.S. Senate seat in California, Muazzam Gill and I accompanied Bruce to one of the Movement's world media conferences in Seoul. In between sessions, I brought Bruce to the same Korean spiritualist who'd predicted my blissful marriage and attempted to get a psychic prognosis on Bruce's electoral chances. The reading came back vague, but Bruce didn't put much stock in that kind of hocus-pocus anyway. Bruce nonetheless thanked Reverend Moon publicly in his conference address for his support years before of the U.S. president Herschensohn faithfully served. Bruce was a man of principle, which endeared him to many. In the end, it cost him with the electorate, who favored liberalism and good intentions to his conservative pragmatism. And in turn, Californians got Barbara Boxer.

Another conservative who took the Reverend up on invitations to speak in Korea was Republican Congressman Robert Dornan of Orange County. An Irish-American firebrand whom audiences (and he himself) loved to hear speak was a frequent guest at the large gatherings the Movement's American Leadership Conference and American Freedom Coalition sponsored. Dornan, an old-fashioned Catholic, "held his nose" in dealing with the Church but nonetheless collected the Movement's honorariums. I once flew with him to Korea with his 20-year-old son. "B-1 Bob," as he was called on Capitol Hill, spoke non-stop for thirteen hours about himself and his accomplishments, never pausing to ask me a thing. Maybe he was still mad at me for my introduction in Anaheim months before, when I suggested to the audience that he was not of Irish decent, but given his propensity to speak beyond the allotted time, possibly a descendant of the eminent Chinese dignitary by the name of "On Too Long." More likely, he was afraid for his son, and didn't want him to hear anything from a former Roman Catholic who'd hooked up with Reverend Moon.

54

A Big Fish
in a Medium-Market Bowl

WHEN I MET RUSH LIMBAUGH, he was a big fish in a medium-sized media market. While pioneering his now-legendary radio talk show format in Sacramento, the large one came to the attention of AFC rep Bob Spitz. Bob convinced me Rush was a rising star and he was afforded an all-expense-paid trip from the Movement to attend an American Leadership Conference in Washington, D.C. Attending with him were other California political figures who were more leery than he was about the Movement's sponsorship of the leadership meetings that attracted some of America's best-known politicians. Dan Quayle, Paul Laxalt, and Robert Bork were among the bevy of conservative luminaries who attended and spoke along with the liberal likes of Al Gore, Geraldine Ferraro and Eugene McCarthy.

Sitting around the lounge late one evening, a female lobbyist from Sacramento caught the attention of Rush. She was as pretty as she was a partisan. And certainly, she was as Christian as she was Republican. He seemed to enjoy listening to the two of us banter about theology and my making fun of her fear that Reverend Moon had invited her to D.C. for an arranged marriage. Rush wouldn't have minded the "match," but he was unsuccessful in converting the perky lobbyist into a gal pal. Then again, it probably would have taken Jesus himself to get a date with that righteous tomato.

Contrary to his on-air persona, Rush is surprisingly humble and gracious in person. Happy to be seated with *Washington Times* Editor Arnaud de Borchgrave, he quietly predicted to the legendary foreign correspondent that everyone in America would soon hear of his radio program. I think that was one of the claims Limbaugh was actually 98.6% right on.

Months later, I had lunch with Rush and political consultant Carlos Rodriguez in Sacramento. Rush wasn't afraid of Reverend Moon or those that had a connection with him. He's the type of person who's secure in his own skin and therefore comfortable with those with different beliefs. After he made it on the national airwaves, I heard a caller ask him to comment on the threat that Reverend Moon posed to anyone associating with his "front groups." Rush spoke positively about his experience at the conference, and how no one had tried to convert him. On the other hand, there's more than a few Unification "dittoheads" in his vast listening audience. In that sense, he did more converting than we did.

As for Bob Spitz, Rush's sponsor at the ALC, Bob was a graduate of USC and went on to become a successful lawyer and judge in Southern California. Bob was the kind of guy that was good to have around. Whenever one of our contacts suggested that all "Moonies were a bunch of brainwashed zombies," I'd point them to Bob to prove the point we weren't all programmed plebes. Hell, Bob once sued the Korean leader in Pasadena over money Bob negotiated from timber sales at the Church-owned workshop site at Camp Mazumbdar. Tough cookie that he is, Spitz has a soft core inside that hard crust. Reverend Moon married him to a Korean woman who endured numerous ailments before passing away. Bob was always loving and protective of her—even when he was his usual ornery self to the rest of us.

55

On the Way Home

SOME OF THE CHURCH'S INSPIRATIONS were so lofty the earthly among us will never attain them. But one idea of the Reverend I connected with was that of a "return to hometown." He himself longed for a return to his hometown in North Korea. The concept was part of the notion that the Kingdom of Heaven itself would be a kind of hometown reunion between God and man. Reverend Moon succeeded in returning to North Korea in 1990 to forgive his jailer, Kim Il Sung. The maniacal dictator even allowed him to visit his family's ancestral home. From that time on, Reverend Moon began to speak to members about going back to their places of birth. Remembering my early musings in Montana about going back to Tahoe, I thought of a way to take him up on the idea.

As it turned out, I was about to get a leader in Los Angeles who would make leaving easier. The man was unusual, even for a Korean. He had a fondness for criticizing people in public and repeating his remarks about them wherever he went. Listening to his sermons was like swallowing fish bones; something always stuck in my craw. And in spite of the fact that the little man in the big pajamas would be upset about my leaving, I remembered the big man's sermons—and began making plans to work my way back home.

As someone who'd never suffered from want of material things in my childhood, I was somehow proud as a Church member of never having a personal bank account until after my thirty-third birthday. Now married with children, Myung-Hee and I opened our first savings account with the kids' birthday money and the nickels and dimes I'd been saving in a Garfield the Cat bank. I keep his plastic countenance on my desk today as a reminder of where we started. With a heart full of hope and a car full of kids, we were ready to go--even though our wallet was on empty.

By the time we made the move, leaders like me had been asked to give up our Church titles and associations and work with a newly formed public lobbying organization called the American Constitution Committee. The group of American former Church leaders was christened the "Africa Mission," because Reverend Moon got everyone to believe we were all about to be assigned to the poorest countries of Africa. All this was before announcing we'd be sent to the deepest, darkest part of the North American Continent–the political realm.

As regional director for the Far Western states, my role was to invite elected officials and other public figures to the American Leadership Conferences held in D.C. Given my new independence from the Church, I orchestrated a move north to Sacramento. Doing so was a step further from the Church structure and a step closer to home. At the time, it was a big stride in Unification circles. No other American in my position had left the confines of the Asian leadership sphere. As much as we venerated Korea for being the fatherland of our faith, the Eastern leaders from the "holy land" could be as difficult to deal with as our Anglo-Saxon predecessors had been for the poor Africans.

My parents were pleased we'd be moving nearer to them. The birth of our four children had done much to make them feel we were family again. Even their initial reservations about Myung-Hee had softened with time. For more than a year after we were matched, they had refused to acknowledge her as a part of the family. She wrote letters, sent gifts and prayed they'd have a change of heart. And eventually they did. Their resistance thawed and my mother sent a one-page note saying, "We have decided to accept you as our daughter." Given the delicious dishes she prepared for them from its starchy seeds, they even were happy I'd married a "rice eater." In fact, my parents' feelings for her changed so drastically, they began to feel sorry for her that she had married me! Grandchildren, as the Reverend predicated, built bridges of love between religions and the races. Confident for the first time that we wouldn't give it back to the Church, my parents gave us a $10,000 down payment for our first home near Elk Grove. We lived out of boxes on the floor of an apartment for the fourth months it took to build it and made it all the more special the day I carried Myung-Hee over its suburban threshold.

Sacramento isn't a bad place to live if you don't mind fog so thick you can't see to drive; or heat so hot you can't get in your car when you want to drive. Our youngest, Hannah, was born there and brought home to the first place we called our own. There the older ones started school and the younger ones stayed at home around the source of all warmth, which was mom. As a mother, Myung-Hee knew how to balance the nurturing the children needed with the self-restraint of not catering to their every wish. The effect was the kids felt secure in love but never dependent on its constant expression.

Many immigrants to this country cling to their own cultural

cocoon. Myung-Hee was different. She made every effort to befriend the parents of the kids' playmates, learn how teachers here teach and even embrace my love of the American sports scene which had become dormant during my days as a missionary. In doing so, the kids have always been comfortable in bringing their friends to a home that didn't smell of kimchi cabbage or look like it was decorated during the Lee Dynasty. These were small concessions to me and the American way of life. But they live large as part of her legacy of loving my country and me, in spite of our faults.

Attending the ALC conferences, I met numerous elected officials from the West. A number of Nevada legislators were regulars. Some, like John Dubois and Bob Coffin, served on the Invitation Committee. Senator Coffin was a rare Democrat who'd been to Nicaragua and didn't believe in the supposed Sandinista makeover that was being touted in the American press. Coffin resonated with the conference's critique and counterproposal to communism and credited Reverend Moon with doing more than anyone in history in identifying the philosophical flaws of Marxism. Sen. Coffin even invited staunch liberals like former Nevada Governor Grant Sawyer to attend. The friend of JFK from Elko was instrumental in removing organized crime from the state and reversing discrimination policies along the Las Vegas Strip. And while the old governor didn't feel compelled to listen to every lecture, he held court in the coffee shop for all of us that were interested. Sitting there chain smoking and drinking coffee, Grant Sawyer discharged both barrels of an active mind at the current follies of the day.

Hearing that I was considering a move back home, Bob Coffin took me aside and talked to me seriously. He explained how the Mormon Church had gained credibility and "muscle" in Nevada through public service and politics. As someone who was attacked in the press for his association with the ALC, he said if the Unification Church was ever to get out from under the cloud of suspicion and controversy that surrounded it, individual members would eventually have to follow the path of the Mormons to gain a measure of acceptance from a skeptical society. Bob was worth listening to. He'd previously advised the ALC to broaden its reach by inviting speakers from both sides of the political aisle. Such advice resulted in Al Gore giving one of his first-ever global-warming lectures at the conference in 1987. Coffin headed up Gore's presidential primary effort in Nevada the following year and I sat in on a meeting with the two of them to discuss the Tennessee senator's aspirations in the Silver State. Personally, I was as doubtful about his thesis on human-caused global warming as I was about his prospects in Nevada; but it was a good political education just being around.

Critics might think the plot to get me elected was hatched in some dark sinister corner of the Far East. But it wasn't a conservative Korean Unificationist who first suggested I run for office in Nevada. Turns out it was a liberal American Catholic who put me up to it, proving that strange bedfellows do get into politics together. And thanks to Baptists like Grant Sawyer and Mormons like Harry Reid, Nevada was no longer the "Mississippi of the West." If any white sheets were being worn in the state by the end of the 20th Century—they were on the queen beds of hotels in Las Vegas and not on the backs of any bigots attacking each other's religion.

When the time was right to move home, I rented an apartment in Carson City behind Paul Laxalt's, Ormsby House. Carson had been my birthplace because South Tahoe didn't yet have a hospital in 1950. Forty years later I was back where things started, beginning life and career anew. Early mornings I'd go across the street to the State Capitol and pray for guidance. Late nights I'd call home to Myung-Hee to be reassured what I was doing was right. On weekends I'd drive over Spooner Pass to visit the schoolyards and the bike paths of my youth. Returning to the Lake, mountain breezes carried the sweet scent of Jeffrey Pines, easily transporting me to an earlier place in time.

56

Live a Life of Conscience

SINCE JOHN FREEMONT'S DISCOVERY of the turquoise blue treasure known previously only to the Washoe, the rich, the famous and the rest of us have stood in awe of Tahoe's alpine wonder. Reverend Moon once visited and got a kick out of the name given the South Shore's ski giant: *Heavenly*. Riding the tramway, the Reverend intuited a mystery beneath the lake that locals already knew. Given Tahoe's frigid depths, many bodies that have drowned there are never recovered and presumed to be preserved at the bottom in an icy locker. Reaching the resort's summit and overlooking its layers of blue and green, he prayed for those souls that were never found.

His soft, caring nature is known by very few. Spending days at a time with him in different places, I've seen it evident in the little things he does in quiet unknown ways. Hearing of him standing on the very spot above my lake, it was wonderful to hear such a story—especially since it took place in view of my boyhood home.

Another such tale is the time he visited the Key West Florida home of Ernest Hemingway. Reverend Moon admired the adventurous author whom he considered a man's-man and who, like himself, was an avid fisherman. Saddened that Hemingway had taken his own life, he tried to buy one of the writer's many cats that still inhabit his waterfront house. The Reverend thought that by keeping one of Hemingway's cats around his East Garden home it would create a connection and a reminder to always pray for the

Skiing with Unification leaders
Heavenly, Lake Tahoe, 1992

deceased literary giant. The attempted purchase was unsuccessful. But if the spiritual world is indeed aware of what we do on earth, then maybe Papa Hemingway was comforted after all by a fellow fisherman.

After moving the family to Jacks Valley outside Carson City, I was invited in October 1992 to go fishing with Reverend Moon in Kodiak, Alaska. By then I was a radio reporter in Carson City and was in the best physical shape of my adult life. I played basketball at lunchtimes at Capitol Courts with a group that included Governor Bob Miller (who, yes, always expected the ball), the Associated Press's Bureau Chief Brendan Riley (whose elbows were as sharp as his exposés) and car dealer Michael Hohl (whose left-handed jumpers were smoother than his commercials). Being in good shape came in handy when fishing with the Reverend. He'd go out before dawn trolling for halibut in Kodiak's saltwater channels only to go back after lunch in search of salmon in the island's freshwater rivers.

After feasting on the catch of the day, we'd sit around on the floor and listen to Reverend Moon into the wee hours of the night. Exhausted from exposure to the Alaskan elements and made sleepy by the crackling fire, most of my fellow disciples dozed off, missing out on the whispered wisdom from the one we considered the Messiah. The same Korean regional director, whom I unceremoniously left in Los Angeles, was there at the North Garden lodge. I worried that he might tell the Reverend about my insubordination, but he kept quiet, seeing that the Reverend had asked me to do the morning scripture reading each day, and may have not wanted to create a stir.

Knowing there would be a chance to speak with Reverend Moon, I was anxious about what he might ask me to do. Remembering my earlier evangelical success in Reno, I thought there might be an expectation for me to be a part of a new pastoral effort in the Silver State. Did he want me to start a Church in Nevada? To my relief, he told me "No." He said there were already enough churches in America. Reverend Moon told me to reconnect with my Catholic roots and "live a life of conscience."

It was the last time I ever spoke with him personally. There was no need to hear any more. That alone was enough homework to last a lifetime.

57

Hang Your Art Where the Sun Doesn't Shine

ONE OF THE FIRST THINGS I did in Carson City was to get a legislative internship with Republican Assemblyman Lou Bergevin from Carson Valley. Given the small gene pool in the Carson Valley, we were probably related one way or another by marriage. Lou was the son-in-law of celebrated Gardnerville rancher Fred Dressler. Once during an interview with Fred, I got off on the wrong foot by asking if he agreed with Willie Nelson's song, "Mommas Don't Let Your Babies Grow Up to Be Cowboys." Old Fred then proceeded to rip me a new one, reminding the listening audience and me that, "I didn't know Willie Nelson (like he did), and I certainly was not enough of a cowboy to know the difference!" That's the kind of curmudgeon Fred Dressler was and the reason why he was revered throughout the West. For decades Fred was afforded a seat at the head of the breakfast table at Sharkey Begovich's casino on Saturday mornings for a free-wheeling discussion with the other movers and shakers in Carson Valley. I was allowed to join once, but was so far away from the conversation I might as well have been the busboy.

Observing Lou Bergevin at the work in the Legislature could be just as fun. Lou had a steel-trap mind for figures and didn't take money or crap from the state's gambling interests. Once he invited me to listen to a call he made to casino mogul Steve Wynn of Bellagio and Mirage fame. Wynn was trying to get the Gardnerville legislator to sign off on his fine-art tax exemption scheme. Lou told the powerful Vegas figure, "You can hang your art where the sun doesn't shine!" That was Lou. And that was the Nevada politics I'd be trying to get myself into.

There were other old Nevadans worth connecting to. Some were relatives. Brooks Park was the family patriarch of the Park Cattle Company. His father, Wallace, had been a Mormon before marrying Maggie Hickey, my father's aunt. She converted him to Catholicism and the Mormons never ended up with access to property at Stateline that would one day turn into Caesars Tahoe and Edgewood Tahoe. Brooks and my father, George, were cousins and fraternity brothers at UNR. They spent their last years together chasing cows on Park Cattle's thousand s of acres near Bridgeport and in the canyon where my cabin would one day be. I joined them occasionally for their regular Saturday-night dinners after Mass with my mom and Brooks's wife, Jean. In spite of Brooks's great wealth, my father always insisted on paying for dinner when it was his turn.

Brooks once told me Dad was one of the few men he'd lend money to without any questions. Of course my Father never asked. Brooks was kind enough to give a friend and gubernatorial candidate Cheryl Lau a generous contribution after our visit to his knotty pine office in the old house on 395. My Dad was driving Brooks the day he had the heart attack that ended the life of one of Northern Nevada's richest men. Brooks Park did it the hard way. Like his lifetime credo stated, "I just put my head down, my butt up, and went to work."

Another old relative was Justice of the Peace James Hickey. Judge Hickey was my father's uncle and the youngest of the Hickey clan that emigrated in the 1870's from County Cork. The first born in America, Jim educated himself on the Hickey ranch by studying McGuffey's Readers and later watching other judges preside over their courtrooms. Justice Hickey officiated over the marriages of the Hollywood likes of Mickey Rooney, Leif Erickson and Jackie Cooper. In all he legally blessed over 16,000 couples in his Gardnerville parlor—most of them before Reno became the divorce capital of the world. In that regard, he rivaled Reverend Moon in the number of people he wed. He just didn't marry them all at once.

Old Jim loved his Model T's, his black Labradors and the people of the Carson Valley. Asked to comment on the future when he retired at 75, Uncle Jim paused and said, "As to the future, right now it's not what I'm going to be, it's what I am now." Here, too, he rivaled the Reverend in wisdom.

58

A Good Face for Radio

KNOWING RUSH LIMBAUGH from my Sacramento days landed me my first radio job at KOH. While interning with Lou Bergevin at the Legislature, Rush made one of his "Rush to Excellence Tour" appearances in Reno. It was in the early days of his show when he still had to create publicity for himself. His visit was big news in Carson City and the *Nevada Appeal* was happy to print an interview that they were unable to get themselves. I asked Limbaugh to comment on the usual issues that people think of when they hear Nevada—like gambling, nuclear waste and prostitution. He answered like someone does who mispronounces Nevada and everything was fine. The station manager at KOH saw the interview and the fact that I worked in the State Capitol and assumed I was a journalist. He called and asked if I'd like to do a daily report from the Legislature.

Before I knew it, I was a Capitol correspondent. Serendipity smiled on this prodigal son. And given that I certainly had a good face for radio and a decent voice to go along with it, the job was a perfect fit. I was at the Capitol every day anyway and with the help of an old Marantz tape recorder given by my friend Muazzam Gill, I got the daily sound bites needed from Nevada's power elite. Writing the copy to go with the interview was an acquired skill and probably the reason why at times you find reading this book difficult. For radio, you write like you talk. So if you're having a problem reading what I've written, give me a call and I'll come over and read it out loud. It'll not only sound better; it should make more sense.

Eventually other radio stations got word of what I was doing and for a while I was doing daily reports from Reno to Vegas and most places in between. Even small towns out in the "cow counties" like Fallon and Elko had me on their airwaves. But the one I took the most pride in was Lloyd Higuera's station, KGVM in Gardnerville. Being on the Carson Valley's 3,000-watt flamethrower, I was assured of at least two listeners every morning at 7:00 a.m.; that being my parents. It was a way of staying in touch without phoning home. Even after my mother had passed away and I stopped sending the reports for Reno and Las Vegas, I kept on doing one for Gardnerville. I knew my Dad would be there waiting faithfully every morning for me, just like he'd done 40 years before at the finish line of my ski races.

Newsmakers aren't hard to grab in a place like Nevada. In California you'd have the concentric circles of staffers and power brokers to break through to get an audience. Since Nevada lawmakers are citizen-legislators, there wasn't any paid staff to run interference for them. In time, I got to know every elected official in Carson City. I tried to be fair and let the issues cover themselves, instead of me trying to cover them with my own biases. Given that most Nevada Democrats were more conservative than California Republicans, and some Nevada Republicans more liberal than their Democratic counterparts, there wasn't the polarization that we see in politics today. Nevada lawmakers have always been an eclectic bunch of characters with relationships meaning more than ideologies and party affiliation meaning less than the geographical area they represented.

59

I Got a Pass on My Controversial Faith

I NO LONGER WORE FAITH on my sleeve. Maybe it was out of fear of being branded or the realization that I had more to learn that I had to teach. I did tell one journalist of my Church connection. Considered the Dean of the Capitol press corps, Guy Shipler's office was next to mine in the old Capitol basement reporters were relegated to. Shipler had come to Reno years before to get a quick divorce and never left. A correspondent for *Time and Newsweek*, he covered the Squaw Valley Olympics in 1960 before he began writing on politics. Guy was an Episcopalian who didn't care if someone was a Mohammedan, Mormon or "Moonist"—as long as they were a decent human being. I thought by confiding in him there would be at least one person in the Nevada press who knew about by background. That way, even if he didn't "have my back," he might at least discourage some other reporter from having my head.

On the night before I was elected, a *Reno Gazette Journal* reporter called to ask where I'd be election night to get my reaction to winning or loosing. After telling her at what casino ballroom I'd be at with my fellow Republicans, she dropped the bombshell I'd been half-expecting. An anonymous fax had been sent to her that day alleging I was a member of the Unification Church. I told her, "Yes I was," but said I didn't see how it had anything to do with the election. She stopped me from becoming defensive and said she wouldn't think of including such an inflammatory fact in an election-eve story. She hung up saying that if I got elected, we might talk about it then. I did. But she never brought it up.

The very religious might say that God took time out of his busy schedule and intervened, keeping her from writing a story. I'd like to think she had good parents and professors who taught her the value of tolerance. Whatever the case, she passed up on the chance for a sensational expose. And I got a pass on my controversial faith.

The incident taught me that it's harder to attack someone you know than someone you don't. I saw that again as the editor of the *Nevada Journal.* One of the cranky writers wanted to include in an article the fact that a certain lobbyist, Sam McMullen, had an expensive crystal collection in his home. Knowing the lobbyist from my days in the Assembly, I figured the writer was suffering from a mild case of class envy. After all, some of the conservative patrons of our magazine likely had crystal in their homes. I persuaded the reporter to stick with criticizing the policy positions of the lobbyist and not his possessions. But, then again, it's easy to cast stones at people that live in glass houses—especially if you've never been invited in.

It wasn't some grand strategy to insulate myself from persecution by being a member of the media, but in some ways it worked to my advantage. Members of the press corps had come to know me as one of their own and not some stranger from a distant planet of faith they knew nothing about except what their Nexus search might tell them.

Sending the kids to parochial school made it tough to subsist on the stipend from the Movement's non-profit arm. The money from the radio reports helped but was not enough to get us in the Catholic classroom unless we were looking for charity. Out of the blue, a Korean acquaintance from Los Angeles came to Carson City and asked if we'd be interested in starting a painting company. Knowing that my relatives were in the construction business, he assumed I had some connections. I did; but I've since learned that family reunions go better when I'm not doing the Hickey cousins' painting.

Carrying the guy's buckets and ladders I could always do, but painting is an acquired skill I'd never mastered. What I did have was a willingness to try something new and the need to do it soon. From years of knocking on doors for a higher cause, I knew at least how to get my foot in the door. In starting a painting business, a little knowledge of paints and how to apply them would seem to be a prerequisite. Possessing neither didn't stop me. While out doing my first estimates, I nodded agreeably to customers in order to appear knowledgeable. Then I'd run to the paint store and ask what the difference was between latex and semi-gloss. For any of our thousands of customers reading this, I'd like to assure you that I know lot more now than I did when I started the business. I've still never painted a house by myself; but I think you'll agree that I've hired pretty good workers that can.

Not being a painter actually helped. My sales and people skills and Myung-Hee's record and bookkeeping talents created a level of management that helped us succeed where other companies who ran their business out of a shoebox failed. The other thing we've tried to do is to treat our employees like family. I wasn't knowledgeable enough to take advantage of them and I sleep better at night knowing I never have. After getting our contractor's license with me as the manager and the Korean painter as the craftsman, the only thing left was to come up with a name for our fledgling enterprise.

That same week in 1991, we'd just finished holding an American Freedom Coalition rally in Carson with Steve Jorgenson in support of the troops serving in the first Gulf War. Governor Bob Miller and Congresswoman Barbara Vucanovich attended and joined my cousin Phil Sullivan and other parents who had sons serving in the Gulf. Americans were anxious to see that what happened to veterans after they came home from Vietnam not be repeated,

With Nevada Governor Bob Miller and Congresswoman Barbara Vucanovich
Carson City, 1991

and turned out in the hundreds to show their support. As a former Draft resister, moments like that helped me feel like I was regaining some of the patriotism I'd been so sorely lacking in the 60's.

Left over from the day's events was a bright yellow ribbon. My daughter brought it home. It sat on the kitchen table long enough to give me an idea for the name of our first business. Yellow Ribbon Painting was born that spring night. Before long we had a small "cottage industry" beside my "radio studio" and the stacks of kids' bicycles in the garage of our Jacks Valley home. Early on, one of our competitors suggested the name Yellow Ribbon was because we had a "gook" working with us. His attempt to whitewash didn't faze us. We were among the many small businesses in Nevada that survived and prospered during the growth spurt of the 1990's and beyond.

With a small business, our kids were able to attend St. Teresa's. Frankly, I think my parents were surprised that we would send our children to a Catholic school. We even went so far as to have the nuns over to our home for a Korean dinner. They laughed and enjoyed themselves in ways the kids never saw in the classroom. In fact, I found myself liking them more now than when I was a good Catholic. Maybe it was the fear factor and the infamous guilt that a practicing Catholic experiences in the presence of clergy; or maybe it was my years of single devotion and abstinence that made me appreciate their sacrifices. Whatever it was, I found myself loving the nuns in ways that I never could when Sister Mary David was paddling me every week in the Principal's office.

While in Carson, I did something else that prepared me for politics. I coached Little League. Once at a candidate's debate I was asked, what was one of my unique qualifications? I answered, "Coaching youth sports programs." To me, anyone who'd been strong-armed by parental lobbyists and survived the politics of all-star team selections would have been ready to serve in the old Soviet Politburo! And in spite of dealing with parents, including myself, who tried vicariously to recapture the questionable greatness of their own playground past, the kids made it all worthwhile. I even sympathized with the guys on the end of the bench. I don't know if they ever created their own "Goon Squad," but I'm sure they had some choice things to say about my coaching style.

At St. Teresa's, I put together a middle-school basketball team that played in the rural school league. Meeting principals like John Prida of Yerington made you wish every teacher took a page from his book. We went as far away as Mineral County to play the Eagles from the Schurz Indian School. They were like us, with too few players suited up, and therefore didn't mind that I subbed my seven-year-old son, Daemin, in the second half. Daemin was one of those insatiable gym rats that ran out on the court during halftimes throwing up a ball that was bigger than him. The extra practice during time outs paid off. Daemin played basketball in college. Back in Schurz, both teams split a gut as Daemin dribbled circles around the plump Indian boys.

That was small-town America in the middle of the Nevada nowhere and you could still find it in the early 1990's. *Hoosiers* had nothing on us. We even played in a gym that looked just like theirs when we went every Easter to a tournament out in Loyalton, California, with Mitch Woods, Teo Gamboa and the boys.

Our Jacks Valley neighborhood was one of those almost-rural places in Nevada with unpaved streets and few zoning restrictions. Our neighbors to the right raised long-haired show rabbits. Daemin and their daughter managed to drown a couple of the critters, seeing if a hare could swim. The family to our right had a Dad who was more mischievous than the kids and took our brood on long hikes looking for snakes, lizards and lonely pine trees on top of nearby mountains. There in on our sandy two-acre backyard, Myung-Hee planted her first garden and harvested enough zucchini to supply Northern Nevada's food banks for a season. Behind the house, Myung-Hee's older brother built a miniature soccer field and backstop for the boys to endlessly kick their ball against. International spectacle that soccer is, it was not my idea of what the boys should be spending all their time at. I built a pitcher's mound in the middle of the field with a 2 x 4 piece of wood as the rubber and a five-gallon paint lid as home plate 46 feet away like Little League would one day be. I spent hours with our oldest, Johnmin, pitching to imaginary batters just like I'd done as a boy at the Lake. By the time Johnmin was10, he was throwing strikes and would continue to do so throughout a successful high school and college career.

Life in Jacks Valley was a long way from the pressures of college or professional careers. It was a time for the six of us to make snowmen, build bike jumps and enjoy enough dusty street memories to last forever.

With the plan for the kids to eventually attend Bishop Manogue

High School in Reno, we moved north of Carson City to Lakeview Estates and bought the home of the pop-singing duo, Captain & Tennille. It wasn't the palatial spread on Franktown Road, but an in-between place they'd built waiting for that mansion to be completed. It did, however, have a master bedroom closet so large we thought of converting in into a bedroom for Daemin. Fearing that two boys living in the same room might one day make us witnesses to a double homicide, we survived for the time being with two kids in each bedroom. With two acres and a long sloping driveway, the Lakeview house was perfect for sledding, roller-blade hockey and enough land for our giant Labrador, Coco, to easily escape. The 125-pound Coco was the kind of rambunctious animal you'd see dragging a child down the block when they tried to take him for a walk. Still, kids that are blessed with an outside to play in are truly blessed to grow as children should. Toys weren't as necessary when you had rock piles, a meadow with a brook and an occasional coyote wandering through your front yard.

60

God Almighty Filed for Office

BESIDES REPORTING ON THE WEIGHTY issues of the day, I also ended up covering a number of quirky characters, which Nevada has an abundance of. On such story was the on the day of May 14, 1992, when I reported on the fact that God Almighty had filed for office in the Silver State. My radio report went like this...

> Many Americans are happy that H. Ross Perot has stepped down off the corporate ladder to run for president. But one individual from Reno is about to top him. And if he is who he says he is...then U.S. Senator Harry Reid may be about to meet his Maker this election season. That's right. "God Almighty" has filled to run for Reid's Senate seat. And in case you're wondering—he's a Democrat! He's 56 years old and his other earthly name is Eli Tolotti. Tolotti was allowed by the Secretary of State's office to file under the name of "God Almighty." State law allows candidates in Nevada to place on the ballot the name they are known by in the community.

Tolotti is reported to have filed for the Senate office in the presence of a friend who swore before God (or his friend) the Reno man has been calling himself "God Almighty" for years. In past elections Nevadans have been able to vote for "none of the above" without fear of retribution. Now one has to wonder what "God Almighty" will think of a vote for "none of the above." But on second thought, why would "God Almighty" want to join the U.S. Senate with 99 others who already think they are Him?
From the Carson City News Bureau for Reno's News Station AM 630, KOH–I'm Pat Hickey.

By the way, in spite of my higher connections, "God Almighty" declined to be interviewed.

There were other such important matters of state like my accidental discovery of Nevada's nude beach, Carson Valley bureaucrats walking on hot coals and the tale on two disgruntled prison employees who proposed opening a prostitution theme park. A reporter's knowledge of the brothel industry actually came in handy when I ran for office. A just-elected state senator had put forth a bill in his first term to outlaw the world's oldest profession. The senator held a press conference to announce his righteous intentions. The problem was, George Flint, the Brothel Association's lobbyist, showed up holding a cancelled check that the senatorial candidate had accepted from the brothel industry during his campaign. Case closed; senator embarrassed.

When I ran for office, I got the same $500 contribution and recognizing the acronym it was sent under; I mailed it back to George with a note saying, "Thanks, but no thanks." I didn't plan on trying to shut down the cathouses during my first term in the Legislature, but I felt good about rejecting the help of at least one of Nevada's legalized vices.

Ross Mitchell, who's been on KOH almost as long as Tad Dunbar has on local TV news, is Nevada's undisputed king of sarcasm and innuendo. One day I reported on the efforts of a local mom to get a life-size cutout of Madonna adorned in lingerie removed from the children's section of a local Penney's Store. Ross introduced my report by saying, "Hickey covers Madonna!" That was Ross and that was the price you paid when you weren't quite a "Boy Named Sue," but had a last name like Hickey.

Another arrow missing in my journalist's quiver was the lack of any formal journalistic training. So when the Editor of the *Nevada Appeal* asked me to do a weekly column on the Legislature, I figured it was a good time to return to school. I applied to the Masters Program at the Reynolds School of Journalism at the University of Nevada, Reno. Political friends Paul Laxalt and Sig Rogich wrote letters of recommendation and before long I was back in school learning to write to be read and not to be heard. "Critical thinking" is the first commandment of a modern J-school education. Being around enough politicians, I had all the ammunition needed to be critical. Time in the classroom would give the chance to do some thinking.

Every semester at UNR, Pulitzer Prize recipient Warren Lerude puts on a "Media Leaders and Management Seminar" and invites working professionals from the media and politics to talk about the nuts and bolts of the business with his students. One such professional was my old adversary from the *Sagebrush* days, Robin Joyce. The strange thing was I didn't recognize him as the author of the scathing article that tried to prevent me from speaking on campus. Years later I stumbled across the story with his byline and my eyebrows shot up! By then Robin had become a friend and campaign manager, but never had brought up the incident that put us at odds ten years before. Call it grace or selective memory; I'm still not sure.

In the year I wrote "Capitol Clips" for Carson City's *Nevada Appeal,* I was edited only once; in my very first column. I made the mistake of mentioning that I was proud to be paid roughly the same amount Mark Twain had 132 years earlier writing on the antics of Nevada lawmakers for the *Territorial Enterprise.* While I was free to attack greedy politicians and goofy bureaucrats, the powers-that-be in the editorial office didn't think it was funny to point out how little a first-time columnist is worth. It's probably about the same as a first-time author—as I'm about to find out. Still, there were plenty of other political ironies to write about at the time.

Any attempt by the press to illustrate what fools Nevada lawmakers can be should begin and end with Mark Twain. Twain and his drinking buddies began a tradition in the 1860s of an "occasionally witty burlesque on legislative life." Called the Third House, it convened when the real House closed business, poking mercilessly at legislators' foibles. At one of the first such sessions, Twain went so far as to call one male senator a "snuffling old granny." I believe it's safe to say that Mark Twain's sense of humor was greatly enhanced watching the Silver State's legislators perform. As he's reputed to have said, "Nevada lawmakers meet every two years for sixty days. Nevada taxpayers, however, would be better served if they met every sixty years for two days!" It was true then and is true now—if you observe the current crop trying to solve the state's financial crisis. I don't know how many readers shared my observations of the Session I reported on, but my job was safe as long as I didn't bring up my pay grade.

What I did mention were items like a poster in the Nevada Department of Education, which read: "Do your employees need to improve their writing skills?"

And incidents like the freshmen from Las Vegas who told the tow-truck driver, "You can't tow my car, I'm an assemblyman!" I reported on the appointment of Vegas casino mogul Steve Wynn's to the Tahoe Regional Planning Agency and the Carson supervisors' hope that "he would have some great ideas for access improvements to Carson City's east shore of the lake." My suggestion that Wynn would probably propose locating a pirate ship in Secret Harbor elicited an angry call from the P.R. person at Treasure Island. I was there the day Assemblyman David Goldwater gave the '95 Session its most memorable quote. Following testimony on the ill-fated bicycle-helmet law, Goldwater uttered the now famous phrase that was posted on bulletin boards around the Capitol: "It's almost my God-given right as a Nevadan to act like an idiot if I want to." Goldwater was right and he was in good company in the Legislature.

One of my favorites was a lobbyist by the name of Ambassador Merlin II. If it sounds like he should represent an extraterrestrial constituency, he did. And along with the Southern Nevada lawmakers who joined his coalition on the earthly plain, he managed to get Highway 375 designated as the EXTRA TERRESTRIAL ALIEN HIGHWAY. Merlin also pushed for Nevada to build embassies for visiting E.T.'s. I thought the measure had merit, especially if the flying saucer visitors leave their money in the state like everyone in Vegas does.

A journalist's prerogative allowed me to follow around a Nevada figure that was very much of this world. He was Supreme Court Justice Cliff Young and I reported on a day in the life of the legend. His career read like a civics lesson with a sagebrush twist. He served in World War II in the 103rd Infantry Division, attended university in Reno and graduated from Harvard Law School. He came back to Nevada and served as a county administrator, was elected to Congress, then spent 14 years in the State Senate before becoming President of the National Wildlife Federation. That was all before he became a Supreme Court Justice.

The best part of the day spent with Nevada's true statesman was the early morning feeding of the striped wild ass on his property that was a product of an encounter between a burro and a zebra. Young's best quip came late in the day during our ride back to Reno through the still-beautiful Washoe Valley. He mused that, "Politicians are people who are allergic to unpopular opinions." And while his opinions from the bench may have been unpopular to some, Cliff Young was the kind of person you could never be allergic to.

Besides reporting on the faces that everyone knew in Nevada politics, there were those who went about doing their daily jobs with little or no fanfare. Persons like Penny Sparks, the nice lady on loan from the Highway Patrol, who chaperoned school kids and visiting dignitaries on tours of the Capitol. Penny said what the kids like best about legislators is that, "They get to call a recess whenever they want, and it always lasts longer than it's supposed to." Observing perks like that, those kids are liable to grow up and become politicians!

Speaking of nice, there was no one kinder than Secretary of State Cheryl Lau. Cheryl was elected Nevada's first Asian-American to a statewide office in 1990. Originally from an old Hilo Hawaii family, Dr. Lau had been a music professor before becoming a lawyer. Cheryl came to Nevada as a Deputy Attorney General where she met her future husband, Garth Dull, director of the Nevada Department of Transportation. I first met Cheryl at an ALC Conference in D.C. when I still lived in Sacramento. After moving to Nevada, I interviewed her numerous times and found that she set the bar for ethical behavior way higher than any state official I'd ever met. Cheryl didn't go unnoticed by the National GOP, who had her play a prominent role at the 1992 National Republican Convention. There in Houston, Newt Gingrich observed her rising star and appointed her General Counsel to the U.S. House of Representatives during the "Contract with America" period. Garth is an avid hunter and outdoorsman and went to D.C.

with his wife. I wrote in my column at the time that I worried he'd find more turkeys inside the Beltway to shoot than he ever did on Western public lands.

In the years since, Cheryl has continued to serve her community in countless ways. A devout Roman Catholic, we attended a Movement-sponsored religious-freedom conference in Berlin. Speaking to the gathering, Cheryl observed that, "Religion may be the most powerful and yet seriously unexamined force this century." I went on to a similar gathering in Tokyo, thinking about what Cheryl had said. Visiting America's two former enemies, I couldn't help thinking about what the United States did after WW II. Historically after war, "to the victor, goes the spoils." America behaved differently after the defeat of Germany and Japan. Instead of ruling, the United States rebuilt. Instead of being punitive, America was magnanimous in victory. To Cheryl's point, I wondered how Judeo-Christian principles like "being your brother's keeper" and "forgiving your enemy" had played a part in the post-war policies of the Marshall Plan and MacArthur's democratization of Japan.

Cheryl was asked to run for a Carson City Assembly seat in 2008. Good Republicans convinced her she was their only hope. I'm guessing her inherent graciousness made it hard to say no. Her elderly parents were both ailing in Hawaii at the time and she shuttled back and forth, caring for them throughout the campaign. After the loss, like almost every Republican in the year of Obama, I felt like telling her being a good daughter was more important than being a good assemblywoman. But I'm sure she already knows that. That's why individuals like a Cheryl Lau are the best of persons, even when they aren't always the best politicians.

David Humke was a Republican Assemblyman and attorney who'd been to one of the ALC conferences. Dave invited me for lunch at the old Pioneer Casino near the Washoe County Courthouse, where he'd been trying a case. He'd heard about my plan to move to Reno to be closer to Bishop Manogue High School, and asked me to consider running for the Downtown Assembly seat. The seat had traditionally been held by Democrats, but he said I could overcome their registration advantage if I worked hard enough. David didn't know he was speaking to the son of George Hickey and hard work was in my blood. Humke's invitation struck a chord and coincided with the advice I'd received from Sen. Coffin and others. Having reported on the Legislature, I knew what I'd be getting myself into. And still I did it.

It meant leaving our Lakeview home and moving into a tiny house near Little Flower School, which the kids would be attending until they started high school at Manogue. With only one bathroom and our oldest sleeping in a converted tool shed, the family made the sacrifices required for me to chase a dream.

Humke recommended John Moore to run my campaign. John, a registered Democrat, knew the district and had managed the campaigns of Bill Raggio, Nevada's Senate Majority Leader. After meeting with Moore, he suggested I use Robin Joyce to help design my campaign literature. I remembered Robin from Warren Lerude's class but not from his days as my Unification naysayer. Everyone involved in the campaign knew of my church connections, but agreed I'd established my credibility as a reporter and businessperson and could weather the storm. The fact that I was from a fourth-generation Nevada family would help shield me from charges of being a carpetbagger; although the Democrats made a weak attempt to do so the last week of the campaign.

Timing is everything in politics. There was an open seat and it seemed that I was ready. Next I would find out if the voters in the district were ready for me.

61

Walking for an Office

BEING A POLITICAL CANDIDATE isn't that different from being a religious missionary. Both require faith and a thick skin. Being a religious representative, your "product" is invisible. As a candidate, you appear in the flesh for the voter to either accept or reject. My Church experiences taught me that being pushy is not your friend. If you want someone whom you have just interrupted either cooking dinner, watching TV or making love to their wife to embrace your reason for showing up at their doorstep—you'd better have a good reason. Going door-to-door for God or for man, it's best to bring along sensitivity as a sidekick or be prepared to get dropkicked off the front porch. A candidate with all the answers and bound and determined to tell someone so while their lasagna is burning, is certain to have his own pasta cooked on Election Day. I wanted my visits to be a pleasant experience and not just an opportunity to preach on all the wrongs I'd right if they just gave me their vote. Anyway, if you talk long enough about your policy positions to a potential voter, you'll give the person a reason not to vote for you.

I asked the friendly folks if they wouldn't mind me leaving a campaign sign in their front yard. The result was I had blocks and of red, white and blue Pat Hickey signs in my Southeast Reno neighborhood. Seeing my signs adorn the streets bringing the kids home from school embarrassed them but made me work harder to validate the support that people had given.

Visiting homes in my District in the afternoons after work, I looked forward to meeting anyone that was home. Some of the old folks just appreciated a visitor, someone who'd listen to their stories and take the advice they'd freely give. I did give the voters and myself a break on Friday evenings remembering how upset I used to get when the Swanson frozen food guy would show up on the doorstep when Myung-Hee and I were getting ready to go out on the town.

Rewards came from helping folks like Mario and Gloria Frediani on Cordone Avenue. They were having neighborhood noise problems from the nearby Kietzske Boulevard car dealer's public address speakers constantly squawking at salesmen to come to the showroom floor. When I visited manager Joe Scalia at Reno Dodge about the problem, he thought I was there as part of a shakedown to get a contribution, which is what he was accustomed to from local politicians. I told him I didn't come for cash but to ask for a little peace and quiet for his neighbors. Surprised I didn't want money, Joe promised to cut the speaker wires himself. In return, I got the thanks (and probably the votes) of the mostly Italian neighborhood. By then I was Mario's friend and eventually painted his house and had him and Gloria appear on one of my television commercials.

To the everlasting embarrassment of my four children, I once brought along the whole family to walk a precinct with me one Saturday afternoon. The poor attempt at campaign overkill ended when I realized our brood looked like a bunch of Jehovah's Witnesses descending on the neighborhood. The kids were relieved and quickly retreated. I'm sure my constituents were also glad. If I'd have kept showing up with all six of us, they may have thought my children were going to go hungry if they didn't "hire" me in November. Nevada taxpayers already had enough drain on their pocketbooks without having to feed my four chow hounds. I hope my children will one day forgive my zeal. Even if they do, they'll certainly never forget it.

Inheriting my Father's work ethic and my years of church-training combined to make me a formidable campaigner. My Democratic opponent, Bonnie Shultz, was caring for an elderly mother at home and had little time to walk the district. I visited every house (with the exception of those with Pitt Bulls in the front yard) in all 23 precincts. Because of it, even though the registration numbers favored her, Bonnie never really had a chance against me. But I didn't know it until after everything was over. I also didn't know what a nice person Bonnie was until we met at an eleventh-hour debate. In retrospect, I was glad I didn't know her. It was easier to campaign against an imaginary foe.

Something else from my past that helped was my ability to fundraise. Merely believing you're a candidate whose time has come means as much as getting dealt a joker in Blackjack, if you can't raise the money to get your message across. Speaking of gambling, the Nevada casinos do bet on elections. Given that odds always favor the "house," gambling interests frequently bet on both "blue" and "red." Like roulette, one of the two is bound to win. Following the election, you could be assured the gamers would be there to cash in their chips when an important bill came up for a vote. I got contributions from the casinos and other business interests. My opponent got most of hers from unions. In the end, I raised more money than any freshmen lawmaker in the North that year and it was enough to spend on the mailings and media needed to win.

Holding a "St. Patrick's Day Mixer" at Reno's Rapscallion Bar in the district gave me a chance to meet the other Pat Hickey in town. A well-known golf-equipment supplier and former rock musician, Pat and I sat down at the bar to toast our namesake and the irony of our meeting. After getting elected, I was happy his name was in the phone book next to mine. That way, he got some of those late night angry calls over a vote I'd made, instead of me!

As much as conservative Republicans liked to dump on the liberal editorial polices of a Gannett paper like the *Reno Gazette Journal,* they were happy if they got its endorsement. I was. The paper said I had "by far, the best approach to problems." A copy of the editorial endorsing me of course found its way into my final mailing.

On Election Day, Myung-Hee and I went early to the polls and even earlier to the prayer tree in Idlewild Park. By then I'd done everything I could think of. For a first time candidate, Election Day is by far the longest day of your life. To make it through the day, I went around to elderly folks' homes in the district and drove them to vote. The best part of being a state legislator was the campaign itself. Later, the questionable ingredients that went into the "sausage-making of legislating" were nowhere near as pleasant.

By the time the polls closed on November 5, all that was left to do was to sit and wait for the results to trickle in. As bored as the kids seemed throughout the campaign, they nervously gathered around the television with us and watched the local news. The first blurb on the screen had my opponent up by a few votes and triggered worried looks from the Hickey clan. I remained quiet, believing that all my visits to the neighborhood would pay off. Which was true and I won by a couple of percentage points. A prayer of thanks was offered and I made my way to the Republican election party to join the legislative fraternity of unusual characters that Mark Twain made so much fun of.

The next day I went around and left a green plant with all those who put up my campaign sign in their front yard. That way, even when my flash-in-the-pan political career ended, I had at least given voters a little shade and a living memory of the time they helped me.

62

My Protector Wasn't Religious

DECENT INDIVIDUALS IN THE PRESS had let my sleeping faith lie. I was more surprised when the Democrats didn't make an issue out of it. They would have, except for a guardian angel of sorts.

My protector wasn't religious; but he shielded the hind side of one who was. Dr. James Richardson is a distinguished sociologist of religion and also the Director of the University of Nevada's Judicial Studies Program. Besides his ivy-covered credentials, Jim is a prominent Democrat in Nevada who once served as Chair of the State Party. Considered an expert on new religious movements, Professor Richardson is frequently called upon to testify on such matters. I'm told a small delegation of Democrats visited his office during my campaign with the newfound knowledge that "Pat Hickey was a member of the Unification Church." Hoping for advice on how to use it against me, they apparently left disappointed. I say "apparently," because I never heard the account from Jim himself. Years later, a Democratic lobbyist told me that when Jim was asked on how to attack my unpopular

religion, "Professor Richardson smiled and showed them the door."
Once again, I was helped by the grace and goodness of someone I
never sought it from.

Christ talked about those who will get their rewards in heaven
because they didn't seek them on earth. The fact that Jim never told me
of the incident probably qualifies him that way. American poet Edgar
Guest once said, "I'd rather see a sermon than hear one any day." James
Richardson wasn't a preacher. But he practiced a damn good one on
that fateful day for me.

63

Life in the Lower House

BEING SWORN IN BEFORE FAMILY and friends is a day worth remembering. What I also remember is that for the first few weeks of the session we practiced the old military drill of "hurry up and wait." Nevada's territorial roots are evidenced in the fact the legislators only meet every two years in Carson City. As Twain smirked, even that often may be detrimental to the well-being of the state. The session is supposed to be for a period of only 60 days. "Supposed to" being the operative word; because 60 days turned into six months—with the bulk of the bills being held to the end of the session when they attract less public attention or are more easily amended when deals are being brokered and legislative horse-trading is being done. In the meantime, we waited and acted important, as only legislators can.

When you're a freshman lawmaker in a minority party there's not much legislation you can expect to get passed in your first session in office. I knew that from my days as a reporter, and didn't bother wasting trees or the time of the Legislative Counsel Bureau drafting up a bunch of bills that I knew wouldn't go anywhere. Instead, I concentrated on preparing myself for committee meetings with, I hoped, intelligent questions to ask. Acting intelligent, or actually being so, isn't a prerequisite for being a Nevada legislator. Nor does it have anything to do with changing or stopping a bill the other party is determined to pass. It gains you respect, or at least some ink from the press, who need someone in opposition to give their story a flavor. Asking questions also keeps you awake in those hot afternoon committee hearing rooms after you've had too much to eat with your lobbyist friends at lunch.

The one piece of legislation I did agree to sponsor came from "the mouth of babes." The "gifted and talented" students from Vaughn Middle School in my district had previously raised money to restore the flag from the USS Nevada battleship that survived Pearl Harbor. They now wanted to see if they could pass a law that did some good. Who could say no to a bunch of seventh and eighth graders who were prepared to participate in the political process? Their idea was to change state law to require only a single license plate, on a vehicle's rear bumper.

The contingent of kid lobbyists knew legislative protocol and prepared their arguments better than most of the so-called adults that appeared before us. The eighth graders struck fear in those that opposed them. The police, prison officials and the 3M Company all seemed nervous being confronted by a bunch of adolescent adversaries. The students' well-researched rationale was that 19 others states required only a rear plate. They testified that doing so would save the state money by having to make fewer license plates. District 27's best and brightest argued that Nevada could also make money from the commemorative plates the state could sell for the front bumpers.

I expected the police agencies to oppose Assembly Bill 449. Better chance of apprehending criminals with both license plates; or so they said. Even the 3M rep's opposition was understandable, since their sale of chemical sealants would drop if the law changed. But when I got button-holed by a representative of the prison system telling me it would hurt prisoners' "take-home" pay, I thought I'd finally seen in my lifetime an example of the inmates running the asylum. It didn't matter that it would save the taxpayers millions, only that it would hurt the bottom line on a felon's paycheck.

Despite the deferential treatment received by the students, their measure went down in flames before the Transportation Committee. After all, the gifted kids from Vaughn Middle School got a good lesson on how government works. And so did I.

There exists a mindset within the culture of government, a near-religious belief that programs for those in need can and should be created; and businesses can always be taxed more to pay for them. The result being the road to the Nanny State is paved with the best of intentions—even though it ends up with potholes and pitfalls too expensive to repair. The oft-used cliché, that "every lawmaker needs to have made a payroll before being elected," makes sense if you believe government should behave like a business. Or if you think government knows how to run a business.

The financial collapse of 2009 would indicate that both government and business have taken those axioms literally. The dalliance between a growing government and greedy business has produced an offspring that is literally eating its "parents" alive. The question facing us all is, "What to do?" America's European ancestors' solution was to flee to a New World. We don't have that option unless global warming has opened up a new frontier in Antarctica I don't know about.

Another thing I didn't know about was how vested the press's interest was in obtaining access to public-employee records. A bill to do so (AB 289) was hotly debated during my time on the Government

Affairs Committee. The Nevada Press Association's lobbyist pursued a broad range of changes to existing law in the name of the "public's right to know." It was assumed that since I had been a journalist, I would side with the press in trying to gain greater access to public-employee records. Aware of how "public figures" are fair game, I didn't think the same distinction should be applied to someone who is merely employed by the "public." In the end, a compromise was reached, which is what usually happens in the legislative process. I don't think the Press Association's lobbyist ever forgave me for being a turncoat. But it served as one of my best memories in the Legislature. After all, I'd been elected to serve "the people" and not just the industry I'd once worked for.

Someone else I was proud to have "worked for" was Lynn Hettrick, the Assembly Minority Leader. Minorities in elected bodies are most effective when leadership rides herd on its members to keep them in line. A determined minority voting block can throw a wrench into the plans of an otherwise dominant majority. Hettrick understood his role with the Republican Caucus. Still, when asked for advice on which way to vote, he would always say, "Vote your conscience." It takes a person of conscience to say that and mean it. Lynn was such a person and such a leader. It's not surprising he called it quits before term limits required him to.

In politics, most just go along to get along. Consequently, there were times that I voted against the flow and against my own fundraising prospects for the next term. In those moments of casting a lone vote, I felt like being stranded on a deserted island. Times like that, I felt my loneliest in the Legislature. Times like that, I felt most true.

Myung-Hee was supportive and ran the business in my absence. It didn't help our company's bottom-line with me missing in legislative action. But that is the kind of sacrifice every Nevada lawmaker's family makes while he or she is off doing a full-time job on a part-time salary.

When the six-month Session finally ended, the majority of legislators never wanted to see the inside of the Capitol again. The feeling would pass, and eventually members would kick back into the campaign mode and get reelected the following year.

I got high grades from the press and everyone expected I'd be back for another term. I had planned to run again. I even sent the first campaign salvo in the form of a survey to my constituents with unused campaign funds to gage my district's views on the issues for the following session.

64

A Change of Colors and a Change of Heart

AUTUMN THAT YEAR BROUGHT a change of colors and a change of heart. Along with the pride in my new profession was the undeniable sense I was missing out on something. I thought of all the people and events in my life that helped me get elected. From my high school pal in Hawaii who predicted it, to my Teacher who let go the reigns for me to return home to pursue my dreams; I couldn't get away from the realization that it was others that had made it possible. There were the legislators from both parties and political friends who mentored me and stuck their necks out in support. There were the members of the press who left me alone. There were the residents from my modest Southeast Reno district who gave me their vote, which is the same as giving me their trust. I often saw their faces while sitting in that expensive leather hot seat the taxpayers paid for in the Assembly Hall.

It was odd to be having second thoughts about continuing. But I knew every year would mean either another campaign or another session. Realizing there wouldn't be time for much else in between, I began to question if it was all worth it.

The problem wasn't with what I was doing, but what I would be missing. My oldest son was a budding sports star, and I wouldn't be around to see him shine. My second son was growing up in his shadow with little time or support from me. My two daughters would never be "daddy's girls," if dad wasn't there to see them off to the prom. Even believing as I do, that life and relationships go on for eternity, being an absentee father during the teenage years of my four children seemed like a poor trade-off for a career in politics. For someone who wanted nothing more than to live with the large family I never had, it didn't make sense to give up that God-given opportunity to be a parent of one.

Shinae, Johnmin, Daemin and Hannah
Thanksgiving, 2008

On the night I sat down to speak with Myung-Hee about my dilemma, something Jesus once said came to mind, "For what will it profit a man if he gains the whole world and forfeits his soul?" I thought to myself, what profit is there in enjoying a measure of prestige if it means loosing touch with my family, which is akin to my soul?

Myung-Hee kept silent as I spoke. She had never complained during the campaign or my time in office about what a burden it had been to care for the kids and the painters in our company. There were times when I'd call her during a break from a committee meeting and find her asleep in the van waiting to pick one of the kids up from soccer with only 20 minutes left to deliver a painting estimate before getting the littlest ballerina off to dance. I knew it was hard on her to see the business decline and the financial strains it placed on the other families that depended on us to help them earn their livelihoods. More than any of those external factors, I knew Myung-Hee would be happy to see that family came before any fame or even the duty of being an elected official. If there is a more important job than being a parent, it seemed it wasn't being a state legislator.

It had meant a lot to gain the office. It meant even more to have had the privilege to serve in it. Still, someone else could fill my Assembly seat. No one else could fill my shoes as a father.

After I'd made my decision and told the leaders of the Party I wouldn't be running again, I felt both sad and relieved. Sad that I couldn't build on the experience I'd gained in my first term; and relieved that my family wouldn't have to face the inevitable rigors of an endless campaign. And while the matter of my Church membership had never come up, there was no guarantee it wouldn't have in a future race against an aggressive opponent. Personally, I'd always relished a good fight defending my faith and the freedom of religion. I'd enjoyed being on the Phil Donahue Show and countless other programs and being grilled by newspapers across the country from the *Washington Post* to the *Sagebrush*. Still, had my children been subjected to the innuendos and rumors that accompany a political dog fight, it would have been hard to bear for both of us.

In the end, I served one term. In doing so, I joined scores of past Nevada "citizen legislators" over the last 136 years who did the same. They came. They went. And so did I. To the casual observer, my political career was like a small rocket launched from Vandenberg that lit up the sky for a brief moment and quickly disappeared. My short political career had been a flash in the pan. But it was a flash...I'll never forget.

65

From the Frying Pan to the Fire

POLITICS ASIDE, THERE WERE STILL MATTERS of public policy affecting me and mine, in or out of office. When Judy Cresanta, the publisher of the Nevada Policy Research Institute's Nevada Journal, asked me to come on board as the magazine's Editor, I said yes. Despite the much-needed attention my painting business was now receiving, I squeezed twenty hours a week out of evenings and weekends to write and edit. Writers for opinion-based journals don't take kindly to editing for content; so I spent most of my time putting my own opinions in print. Going from being a politician and making policy, back to a writer criticizing politicians and their policies, was a little like going from the frying pan to the fire. Politics provided the heat, the press was the cooker and our policy pieces were the grist that was left when all the sautéing was done. Besides, sticking around the political scene for a while helped me make a recovery while weaning myself off the dependency of being in the public square.

I wrote feature articles on religious freedom, asking whether "freedom of or freedom from was the growing trend." An article on news reporters as news spinners asked the question, "Why have we left the so-called watchdogs of society off their ethical leash?" I authored pieces on education, soft money and cozy relations with Nevada's media moguls. But my favorite was a cover story on how the U.S. Forest Service played fast and loose with a Tahoe land deal with my relatives, the Park family. The juiciest part of that particular expose was the discovery that Nevada Senator Harry Reid had been able to have disgraced Senate colleague Robert Torricelli (D, NJ) stay at the former Dreyfus Estate on Tahoe's East Shore, even though Park Cattle Company couldn't use it themselves as promised by the Federal Government.

Writing did me good. It helped ease my way out of the political arena without having to just slam the door shut. At the same time, I finished the course work at the Reynolds School for my Masters. The thesis involved studying what members of the Nevada Assembly thought about media coverage of the legislature. Having served in the previous Session, I knew most of the members to be interviewed for the study. But since I was editing and writing for the *Nevada Journal* at the time, I decided to resign as editor in "order not to create a possible conflict of interest that would either skew [this] study or make individual members [like yourself] uncomfortable with the interview process."

The result was, members opened up about their views of the media. They talked about "being used" and "manipulating the media" themselves. In the end, there was nothing groundbreaking or extraordinary about my thesis. Most knew who it was I was quoting when I mentioned, "a long-time rural Nevada Assembly leader" said so and so.

Former Nevada Governor Mike O'Callaghan and then-*Las Vegas*

Sun Executive Editor suggested "that every member of the [Nevada] media get a copy of Hickey's thesis and spend 30 or 40 minutes reading it."

O'Callaghan was revered by Nevadans for his candor and accessibility. He has since passed away from a heart attack while attending Mass. He proved his candor in the "Where I Stand" editorial (*Las Vegas Sun*, April 20, 2001) by revealing my connection to the Reverend. But with a person like Mike O'Callaghan, you didn't worry about being "stabbed in the back," because whatever he thought—he said it to your face. He wrote: "Writer Pat Hickey was in town last week and we had some time to visit. Hickey, a former GOP assemblyman from Reno, is one of my more interesting friends. His interest in local, state, national and international politics is the product of an active mind and a broad background. He sided with the Contras in Nicaragua so he went down there and took them needed supplies. The other day he came to Clark County with Rev. Sun Myung Moon as a member of the Washington Times Foundation. If it's controversial or exciting you can find this father of four not far away."

Thanks, Governor, but I was hoping to get away from the secular and the sacred long enough to regain my balance. Like my fictional fellow-traveler Siddhartha, I'd lived fully on both sides of the coin toss called life. No more heads or tails for a while for this Nevadan. Leaving public life, I stuck the lucky penny in my pocket. Besides, there were kids to raise, a cabin to build and a Lake to return to before turning 60 and placing my next bet.

66

Being a Father, Finding God

IF WHAT THE GOOD BOOKS say are true and "God is love," being a father or a mother may be the surest way to experience both. From the delirious joy of a son's birth to the ups and downs of a daughter's adolescence, nothing put me more in touch with the realm of the heart than signing on as a parent.

Compared to the animal kingdom, human children take forever to grow and leave home. Parents spend decades bandaging cuts, grounding their teenagers and paying for schooling and weddings. More than a biological impulse or a societal norm, any parent worthy of the title "mom" or "dad" finds their total being wrapped up in the life of their offspring. Nothing in my past led me through the gamut of emotions that being a parent has.

Like the day Johnmin was chasing Daemin around the Jacks Valley kitchen hoping to inflict retribution for some unlawful infringement on an older brother's space. Daemin slipped and tore his lip wide open on the protruding kitchen counter. Seeing a child covered in blood ripped at something far deeper than his wound. Racing to the hospital, red lights and pedestrians were rendered invisible by the drive to safeguard my son. Who among us can ever understand what the victims of violence feel when the injured party is a child? Even Heaven's tears turned to blood when Gethsemane's prayer pierced the heart of a father. The sun hid itself and the curtain of the temple was torn in two the day sorrow permeated the universe over the loss of such a son.

Thank God, the joys of fatherhood resonate just as far. Sharing what co-creatorship we have in common with God is all the cosmic consciousness this '60's soul will ever need. Becoming a parent provided a glimpse. Being a parent revealed a heart-full.

Like the thrill of seeing my oldest son win two straight state basketball championships at Lawler Events Center and being MVP of both. Being there that moment of his last-second steal and the winning free throws I couldn't bear to watch. Or the delight I felt escorting two different Homecoming princess daughters out at halftime of the big game. And the even greater satisfaction of seeing a stubborn younger son, who'd been kicked off his team the year before, star in the Zone Championship game before gaining first team All-Region honors the following season. Sharing his tears and sending off my impassioned letters to his Principal, gave me the chance to not only wear a dad's heart on my sleeve, but hang it out for a son to see and one day understand. Incidents like that were costly. Earning a son's trust was priceless.

In the quiet after-hours of pillow-talk time, when prosperity is calculated and blessings are counted, it's always in the context of the kids. Every parent learns sooner or later—that there is no greater wealth to be had on earth than the richness of raising children. How fortunate I've been to have four who taught me to love in ways I was never capable of before them.

The irony of how much better sons and daughters they have been, than I was to my parents, is the result of their mother. I'm still waiting for payback time from my 1960's-inflicted karma catching up with a character like me.

My questions now are not as esoteric as they were in my youth. Having children helped change that. My oldest daughter, Shinae, once told me she didn't care whether or not Jesus came to die—she was satisfied knowing how he lived. Shocker! Once more from the mouth of babes comes the truth, just as he said.

Trying to be a good father was one thing. Becoming a better son was just as important. Coming back to Nevada was the first step in restoring my prodigal past. Making up for what my parents thought I squandered took time, as did proving to them that our return home was for good. Not necessarily permanent—but for good, as only a parent can define. Like Jacob needing children and a little wealth to offer the resentful Esau, the family and our minor accomplishments put my parents' minds mostly at ease. Myung-Hee was patient and endured my Mother's wrath until the point that kindness and persistence won over a one-time foe. Being a good mother is enough to convince most grandmothers. Myung-Hee was, and did.

Before her death, my Mom lost most of what she'd relied on. Emphysema claimed her eyesight and ability to get around. My father stayed by her side and cared for her every need. All of us, including my sister Sherrie, were there the day she gave up the ghost. Back from her final visit to the hospital with nothing more that could be done; she sat in her favorite chair able only to hear her loved ones all around. Minutes before she woke up in the next world, I too felt an urge to sleep and lay down on her side of my parents' bed. I think my mother was inviting me to see her off. Later in a dream I saw her freely dancing as a young woman in a field of wild flowers in her next existence. Like it's said, the dead begin rejoicing before those of us left behind start to mourn.

Waking from my nap, I was the first to notice Mom would not be getting up from her chair. My Father cried out for his *"Alynnie."* But it was her time, in her home and with her family all around her. May we all wish for such a peaceful transition to whatever waits.

**With my 96 year-old Dad
Home, 2009**

Everyone worried for Dad. He'd been so totally devoted the relatives all said he'd be one of those husbands to quickly follow after her. Eleven years later and now 96, he hasn't yet left us to join her. In the time he stayed in their home, he walked daily to the gravesite. Even now, when I take him with me to Gardnerville for painting estimates, he visits and has his private little chat with her. I hear him saying he's "sorry" for not being able to do more than change her artificial flowers, which becomes harder and harder for a 96-year-old to bend over and do. But there's nothing synthetic about the lesson on love I'm learning, and maybe the reason he's stuck around so long to teach it to me.

My Dad eventually moved in with us in Reno. He's still going strong. I bring him to the doctor for his annual physical, and Dr. Ryan Gini tells him the same thing every year. "Sorry, George, I just can't find anything wrong with you." During his last visit, Dad let Ryan in on a little secret. He told the Doc it's because of the "vitamin B" he takes every day. Irish translation: a shot of brandy from the jug under the sink. His vitamin supply now resides in our kitchen, like he does in our house—waiting to be tasted and giving off its unique warmth once it is.

The other day he told me he lies in bed in the morning and breathes deeply before getting up. Maybe that's another of his secrets to a long life. I know the yogis are big into breathing, I just didn't know a retired iceman could stumble upon the same wisdom. At any rate, most of his peers are no longer sucking air and he often wonders why he's the only one left. I think he's stayed to give us the chance to show him how much we love him. I've promised to the relatives that his funeral will include a happy Irish Wake. Not many of his contemporaries will be around for it—but they can invite him to one on their own dime when he arrives upstairs.

The cycle of life is a beautiful thing. Our parents take care of us when we're young, and if we're lucky enough to be able to return the favor, we can take care of them when they return to their almost child-like state near the end of their life. Having the three generations together in our house gives a peek into the portal of eternity. The past is there in Grandpa, the present here in us and the kids comprise the future. It occurred to me, that if there is an afterlife, it must include family. But even if life as we know it ends with physical death, family is the best way I know of to live while we're here.

67

Building the Cabin
My Grandfather Lost

ONE OF THE FEW REGRETS MY FATHER has is not having acquired or kept land around the Lake like the Park side of the family did. He remembers his time as a child and the cabin his father built and then lost. I went to Marla Bay recently looking for old timbers or posts but found none. If there were any remnants there, they were buried beneath the snow pack–which is how all good things should be put to rest, under the quiet solitude of a white winter blanket.

I walked in the meadow where my father must have played. It's the same pasture many of you saw the four horsemen of the Ponderosa–Ben, Adam, Hoss and Little Joe of Bonanza fame–ride up on their mounts with Mt. Tallac, Lake Tahoe and the Bonanza theme song in the background.

Coming back to the Lake, I wanted to leave my descendants something more than my invisible heritage of love. I wanted to pass on to them a tangible treasure that could embody the enduring quality of love. Buying land along the lakeshore these days is out of the question unless you're a trust-fund child of Bill Gates or Steve Wynn. Besides, Tahoe is no longer the tiny Ski Run community I peddled my bike around. A sight for a family cabin would have to be found nearby, in the "spirit' of Tahoe, but not in the immediate vicinity of the now condominium culture.

The two of us spent years praying and taking weekend jaunts looking for just the right piece of land. I had grown up by a lake and Myung-Hee by the sea. We compromised on a place with a river, as long as it was running through it. One Sunday after forgoing church as usual for a hike through the meadow near Mt. Rose with a visiting old friend, Joe Tully, I got the idea to call my realtor cousin Phil Sullivan. Phil's wife, Gladys, said he was away on a pack trip with his horses, but she remembered him talking about a property along the Walker River in Mono County. Hearing what might be an answer to our prayers, I grabbed Myung-Hee, got directions from the only realtor in the office and within a couple of hours we had feasted our eyes on the high meadow in Mono and the surrounding 10,000-foot Sierras that encased it. Passing 1,000-year-old cedars, their twisted limbs appeared to be beckoning us on. Creeping up the rocky road to the Forest Service gate, we were about to enter a mountain paradise that only a few hearty backpackers and fishermen had ever seen. It took about 20 seconds for both of us to conclude this was the place of our dreams. We turned around and drove straight back to the Coldwell Banker office in Minden.

Having no prepared savings or plan to finance the dream, we nonetheless wrote a $1,000 deposit check in hopes that it was meant to be. Good thing we did. The next day, another potential buyer made an offer, but ours was first in line. At the gateway to the Hoover Wilderness Area and only about 20 miles to Yosemite as the Red Tail flies, it was land that amazingly was still private in the midst of a wilderness that will never be. I learned from my cousin that the owner was a local Native American from Carson City who had owned the land for years with his mother, a horsewoman who rode into her eighties.

Since Leroy was an Indian, I figured the passing of the land to our family would be more a spiritual matter than a business transaction. Knowing first hand the resentment his race rightfully feels, I determined to find a way to give him whatever he was asking. Negotiation would indicate a deal being sought and not a stewardship being inherited. I think I was right in that regard. When it came time to close the deal, I passed another meadow landowner on the narrow road driving up to see Leroy. I'm told he offered him more than $50,000 in cash from what the seller was asking. Thankfully Leroy was an honorable person and kept his word and the deal with us.

On the day we signed the contract, Leroy took all six of us around the perimeter of the property, sanctifying it with his family's feather and the tearful blessing of his mother. I've since invited him to visit and stay a night with us in the cabin we built on the site he cleared. He's never visited while we're there, probably coming on his own time choosing to remember the land as it was and not as it is now.

Receiving title to something so remote and beautiful does little to make you feel you "own" it. Land like that, in its untouched splendor, can never really be owned by anyone. At best, we're part-time caretakers of a place that belongs to the ages. Still, Mono County, which has more tree huggers and salt lake lovers than most anywhere in the country, gave us a permit to build a small cabin there. More specifically, it's a 588 square foot palatial shack and a place to enjoy the peace of the Sierras like Tahoe used to be. Two miles up the Little Walker, entering Burt Canyon, you pass through an Aspen-domed corridor that welcomes you like you are the first human being ever to have set foot there. At the end of the wild-flowered ravine begins the ascent up the trail to 11,000-foot Anna Lake and its mythical Golden Trout. There you run into a series of Beaver ponds nestled between lone pines that look like little lakes. Wild ducks, newborn fawns and an occasional black bear come there to taste of their clarity and to marvel at the busy beavers and their work.

Fishing along the Walker, it's easy to lose all sense of time and self. Myung-Hee once asked me after returning hours late for dinner, what I "think about" when I'm fishing. I thought about it and said, "I don't think about anything." Fishing transports to a place where thinking in no longer necessary. Every normal habit is easily forgotten. Who needs a Buddhist temple and chants to empty yourself of all thought? Go fishing in the beaver ponds and you will find

Fishing the Little Walker
Mono County, 2005

peace that passes all understanding. Gaze at the shimmering body of a green, red, blue and gold Brook Trout—and in that moment you may find assurance of a Creator.

As God's first Bible, nature can teach us just about everything we need to know. Lectures are abundant seated on a river bank beside a flowing brook. Even my aging dog Sunny, full of arthritis and injuries from skirmishes with bigger dogs, seems free of pain when she roams the land. Her aches return as her joints stiffen up at the end of a day of chasing chipmunks, deer and every bird that catches her eye. But for that time that she's free to be an animal and not a pet, she's seems to forget all pain. I'm the same way. No headaches. No anxiety. No aching joints when I'm along the river. And most importantly—no cell phones to intrude in my far-off corner of the Sierras. Mind and body easily become one with the hope of a rainbow rising to the surface on the other end of my rod. The mind assumes the driver's seat in nature and puts itself on auto-pilot. My tired body goes agreeably along for the ride only to voice its complaints back on the old leather couch in the cabin.

One day near the lower pond I saw a Disney-like Bambi. A newborn fawn so young its legs were still wobbly. Actually, I saw her mother first, which is a better order than the time I saw the bear cub, minus its mom. Unlike the young bear that ran toward its mother, the Doe ran away to draw my attention to her and away from her vulnerable offspring. The spotted youngster eventually saw me and instantly genuflected in the sagebrush and the wild irises, crouching absolutely still. Instinct, not training, had taught it that maneuver. A day or two old, mom had not had time to instruct her on the ways of survival. She didn't need to. Nature provides its own code of instructions to those in the natural world.

Thank goodness I'd brought with me the new dog, Bridget, and not the old gal, Sunny. Sunny will go after everything she sees or smells. She's chased our cousin's cattle grazing on the open range who don't distinguish between private land and the public domain. Sunny would have sensed the fawn—and caught it like she did the sheep the summer before, who dragged her through the river with her jaw attached to its wooly tail. Bridget, who is a French Mastiff, like the slobbering monster Tom Hanks had in *Turner & Hooch*, sticks by me when we fish. Lucky for Bambi, the petrified fawn was not seen by Bridget the "Bordeaux." My lumbering lion look-alike would probably have tried to lie down with her. I saw her do as much one day when I found her trying to cuddle with a stray sheep she thought might have been the mother we took her from. Score one for the natural world. The lions and the lambs are certainly closer to lying down with each other than we humans are at the dawn of the 21st century we occupy.

The cows Don Bentley's buckaroo brings up for a month or two when the meadow grass is green, the sheep herd the Basque run here in summer and the deer that deposit their young among the Aspens on the northwest corner of the property—all were here before us. Hopefully their descendants will still be grazing in Hickey meadows long after the cabin and everything but our ashes are gone.

Despite its cedar siding, the cabin isn't much to look at from the outside. The natural environment didn't need any help from our wilderness design to complement its majesty. Our builder was a local contractor by the name of Gordon Barkley. From nearby Coleville, he'd done work at Park Cattle's ranch near Topaz Lake. Cousin David Park introduced me on a day we were having lunch with my Dad at the Meadow Cliff, where he and Uncle Brooks would go to have soup and a sandwich on cold days after chasing stray steers. Meadow Cliff is where all the Coleville regulars assemble each morning for coffee and a cowboy's version of networking and manly gossip.

Gordon is like most contractors from a small community. He's a great tradesman, a hell-of-a person and slower than molasses. I got to work more that way and got to know Gordon better in the process. If you need help, as I most certainly did in building my Shangri-La—I recommend you find someone like Gordon. Cutting corners is a bad idea if you're trying to put up a lasting structure at 8,200 feet in the Eastern Sierras with snow loads and black bears trying to break down what you've built. Wanting our grandchildren to one day enjoy the cabin with their own kids, we tried to make sure it would still be standing long after we weren't.

**With Muazzam Gill and Myung-Hee
the cabin, 2008**

Inside the tongue and groove walls and ceiling and the fir floor, we added an attic with a makeshift ladder to propel grandkids up to build forts and a general ruckus. A cast iron wood stove makes sure cold nights in May and November remain bearable. A kitchen with a propane stove and fridge makes Myung-Hee's hot trout soup and a cold Guinness always an option. But more than any amenities we managed to include, the cabin is a place to have those lazy summertime conversations on the porch with friends and family gazing up the glacial Yosemite-like canyon in awe of all that God has given.

Nighttimes along the Walker, the Milky Way is so thick it looks like a sparkling throw rug strewn across the summer sky. The evening sky's rich nougat of stars is as tasty to the eye as its chocolate counterpart is to the stomach. The sights and smells of a clear August night combine to convince even the skeptic that something infinite had a hand in designing the twinkling light show above.

I could live forever on the land. The fact I won't, makes it all the more special to return following a long winter away. Future chapters may be written about the Eastern Sierras' biggest little meadow. For the time being, like a favorite fishing hole, the less said the better.

68

The End of My Religion

WHEN I USED TO LECTURE for the Church, the question of whether "all roads lead to God" often came up. The temptation for the average believer is to say, "They don't." But as times goes on, I've become less and less average.

If I ever got anything close to another revelation after that time in Bozeman, it was the on the night of watching the *Wizard of Oz* for the first time since childhood. Maybe it was the addition of Technicolor that brought its symbolism to light. In search of the "way to Oz," Dorothy and her three fellow seekers arrived at the end of the road following their lengthy ordeal. Pulling back the veil that hid the Great Wizard, they saw to their great surprise that the personage behind the curtain wasn't all they'd imagined him to be. They discovered everything they thought only "He" could provide was already within them. Courage was embedded in the will of the cowardly lion. The scattered scarecrow had street smarts. And a heart beat strongly within the tin man whose rusty tears proved it. Watching that televised children's fable, I realized what Jesus meant when he said the "kingdom of heaven is within you."

For someone with so many questions in my youth, I naturally looked for answers where I could find them. Religion is one of those vehicles a person like me gets into looking for safe passage to some big picture destination. For some the choice may be a red sports car that can speed from 0 to 60 in mere seconds down a track of instantaneous gratification to the finish line of bliss. For others, a lumbering sedan with orthodox airbags traveling along the straight-and-narrow highway to salvation is the answer. For me, the black stretch limo of Catholicism brought me only so far. Unificationism picked me up hitch-hiking in one of those innovative Asian models that captivated the market in the 1970's. How far it will take me depends on how long I stay in it.

The institutions religions create easily forget they're just a mode of transportation to get their passengers home to God. Henry Ford would have eventually traded in his first Model T. Jesus turned in his old wineskins and advised us to do the same. Go ahead and keep the '69 Ford Mustang that brought you to your first dance, but remember to park it outside when you enter the King's palace to waltz. The vehicle of one's faith is only the means to an end. Reaching the end in God meant the end of religion for me, or at least the need for its rituals.

The yellow brick road may not be the only way to Oz. But for those of us like Dorothy, what we go through, and what we become along the way, makes all the difference in who we are once we finally arrive.

69

The Tahoe in All of Us

GOING HOME FOR THE GIRL FROM KANSAS was like finding the way back to the Lake for me. There was no place like home and no place like Lake Tahoe, to finally find my peace. Returning, I too pulled back the veil and opened a curtain to the happiness I'd sought ever since growing up there as a boy.

Revisiting Hidden Beach and the unmistakable smell of manzanita, the same senses of my youth were filled by the Lake's indigo charm. The shoreline boulders rubbed smooth by centuries of east rolling waves still sit ensconced in awe in their front row sand balconies. Blue Jays still chatter high above proclaiming their continued dominance. Descendants of the crawdads I once caught wait lurking below their rounded protectors, only to be lured out of hiding by this generation's boys with their dangling chicken necks suspended from a string. Tahoe, with your alpine water so clear the lakefront bottom is no mystery at all. Will you be there as you are for me now when young men come to visit in another forty years?

Tahoe, your turquoise ripples spilling over Secret Harbor's hump back stones made me think for a second I saw a whale surfacing in your shallows. With your snow water still so cold, only on a stormy day when the air is chilled do you ever seem warm to the touch. I see your small fishing boats have returned trolling for trout. They were there before the commercial excesses of the early Twentieth Century and they too have a come back for a peace of the action. Tahoe, your basin is the Sierras' most delicate piece of granite pottery containing God's purest liquid wonder. I pray we will always be able to dip our ladle in into the depths of your beauty.

Your clear waters never reach the Pacific. They have drawn me back like a landlocked Kokanee looking for the fresh tributary of youth to deposit my heritage. The warmer surface water, constantly mixing with the cold aqua below, prevents you from ever freezing. So too will my thoughts and memories always be churning like your blue legacy still running through my veins.

70

The Last Chapter

TAHOE BOYS BECOME TAHOE MEN and eventually wither away. My sand box companion Jon Springmeyer, whose family now owns the old Hickey Ranch, is battling the grim reaper of cancer. A lawyer and a tobacco chewer, Jon probably did too much with his mouth. These days, Jon gets whimsical and compares himself to an old Cottonwood standing tall along the riverbank, hiding the fact it's dying from within. Not to worry, old friend, we're all lined up in that row beside you ready ourselves, to splinter and fall when our time comes. For now, we each provide what shade we can and the living memory for those who stood around us during our brief time in the sun.

At least you were not like your older sister, Constance, who at three years old fell into the irrigation ditch on the old ranch and never lived on the Lake like the both of us did. The small white-picketed plot where your mother Marjorie placed the cherubic statue and the yearly wreaths is a fitting tribute to life's innocence and frailty. I hope the three year-old sister you can't remember and the 58-year-old memory your mother cannot forget, will help prepare for the Johnny's and the Pat's of this world when it is our time to enter hers.

And if this world is all there is, then, we are no less indebted to our sources. But if eternity does await us at the other side of this life, then we'll enter as mere babes in the wood with forever to find just over the next horizon, our beloved Tahoe.

After all, gaining happiness is damn good to do.